CONTROL YOUR CAREER

5 STEPS to Stand Out and Get the Job You Want

SOOZY G. MILLER

CPRW, CDCC, CDP

QUANTUM SHIFT
P U B L I S H I N G

PORT SAINT LUCIE, FLORIDA

For information about special discounts for bulk purchases, please contact soozy@controlyourcareer.net

Editing, cover and interior design by Quantum Shift Media

Paperback: 978-1-955533-37-9
eBook: 978-1-955533-38-6
Library of Congress Control Number: 2025903941

Printed in the United States of America

QUANTUM SHIFT
PUBLISHING
PORT SAINT LUCIE, FLORIDA

DEDICATION

I dedicate this book to my mother and father, Barbara and Mark, who gave me the courage, wisdom, and confidence to try new ideas and use them to serve others.

PREFACE

Every day, I hear these words: "I'm scared." "I'm stressed. I have no idea what to do next." "How do I get a job?"

I get it. You feel stuck.

You need to earn money to pay for life. And you don't want to get any job; you want a job that inspires you and feeds your soul. You want a job that you will look forward to every morning. You want a job where you feel comfortable and the work makes you proud.

We all focus on the Next Big Thing. The next promotion. The next raise. The next job with more responsibility and a higher salary. Consider these questions and answer them as honestly as you can.

- How would your life improve if you lost a job and didn't feel stressed about it?

- How would you feel if you were laid off or your contract ended, and you could simply say, "Okay, next!"

- How would your life change if you felt comfortable and secure enough to calmly, confidently, and intelligently find the opportunity that makes you happy?

- How would your life change if you considered different positions at different companies, perhaps even companies you never thought you would consider before?

Even if you recently graduated, your power to land a great job lies in your ability to demonstrate how you can address the company's needs and make the company better.

Sometimes, clients come to me with a plan, saying, "I want this job. I'm perfect for it. I've worked my whole life toward this goal. This is my dream job!"

And let's say that you land that job, and it turns out to be a nightmare instead of a dream.

Let's say that you hate your boss. Let's say that your predecessor left the place a mess, nobody knew, and now you have a whole mess to clean that you didn't expect.

Or the opposite may happen. You like cleaning up messes; that is your specialty. You were told that you were the perfect person to clean up the mess, and it turns out that the problem wasn't very big. Now, six months later, you're stuck in a maintenance role, yawning with boredom.

Or let's say that you land a unique advisory role because you believe in their mission. Then, a venture capital group suddenly takes over the company, and their only mission now is to bring shareholder value.

There are a lot more scenarios that I could offer. They are all based on true stories from real people.

You want the power to decide what you want to do next with your career.

There are plenty of examples of people who feel stuck in their situation, and believe me when I say that the rest of the company suffers. Even if you're not aware of it, the people around you—bosses, colleagues, and assistants—will sense from you that something is awry. They may not want to say anything about it, but in my experience, company culture and the working environment result from each employee. People who are unhappy in their position, whether or not they realize it, set a tone that reverberates throughout the company.

People of all ages and professions come to me complaining about all kinds of job search challenges:

- Tool problems
- Skill problems
- Location problems
- Job availability problems
- Job gap problems
- Ageism problems

And these problems always boil down to a resume problem. We will fix that.

You can control your career decisions until you no longer want to work. That's why I wrote this book. The tools and methods I give you have worked for many people before you, even during massive layoffs, and for any position. I repeat: Any position.

This book will help you get there. Just follow the steps and use the tools.

I promise you will feel more powerful and more in control of your career when you're done.

My mission is twofold: to improve company culture one person at a time and to show you how to control your career until you decide to retire.

And I'm with you every step of the way.

Soozy G. Miller

ACKNOWLEDGMENTS

I want to thank my fellow coaches, executive advisors, and all the career help agencies with whom I've enjoyed working. I took what worked best with clients and left the rest.

Thank you for your inspiration and your ideas.

I have taken many of your awesome methods and improved on them to give people the power to make better choices about their careers.

I could not have written this book without you.

CONTENTS

DEMONSTRATE YOUR IMPACT

The Problem: Proving You Are the Best Person for the Job

This is the most important part of your job search. Period. During your job search, you need to show on your resume or LinkedIn profile that you're the better candidate and demonstrate why.

But how exactly do you do that?

Impact is the most important part of your resume, LinkedIn profile, cover letter, professional biography, and interviews. It's even important if you have your own website.

Yet, 99% of job search materials are missing impact.

Why?

Most job seekers—from high school graduates to CEOs—look alike in their resume. This is because most job seekers put their skills and describe what they do or have done. They state their skills. They describe their actions. Almost no one talks about the impact of those actions.

The impact is how your actions improved the company or organization. You want to show how your actions, expertise, and skills improved each organization. This appeals to the hiring team.

MYTHS

◆ Hard work and getting the job done will get you noticed.

◆ Passion for your field is an argument for getting hired.

◆ Loyalty is an argument for getting hired.

◆ Your skills and actions are enough of a reason to get hired.

◆ The hiring team has probably never seen anyone like you before.

◆ Your decades of experience make you an expert and, therefore, make you stand out.

◆ Impact is easy to figure out; you talk about it all the time during interviews.

◆ Skills and responsibilities prove why you deserve the job.

Terms Not To Use

Based mainly on the above myths, here is a list of commonly used terms that people have used to get noticed that are not helpful at all:

- Passion
- Good communicator
- Innovative
- Transformational
- Entrepreneurial
- Computer skills
- Detail-oriented

- Organized
- Work well with others
- Dedicated: Put in long hours

So, don't use any of the above words if you want to get noticed.

What Is Impact?

Impact is different. Showing how your expertise and your experience made the company better differentiates you. That's what the hiring team wants to know about. How will you make the company better after you're hired? That information makes you stand out.

You may have received instructions to tell a story about your accomplishments (e.g., STAR, SAR, SOAR techniques), but stating impact can be even easier than that.

The Solution: Write An Impact Statement for Each Position

Let's break down impact statements into two simple parts.

Part 1: State the Impact First

For every statement in the Experience section of your resume and LinkedIn profile, ask yourself:

- How did I add/contribute to revenue?
- How did I improve a process or procedure?
- How did my work benefit a client? How did I make their life easier?
- How did my work save the company time and/or money?
- How did I develop/expand the business?

- How did I increase the customer base?
- How did I improve/enhance a project?
- How did I solve a problem?
- How did I enhance teamwork?
- How did I improve policy? Compliance?
- How did I influence someone to make a better decision?
- How did I use data or research to improve something or solve a problem?

The answers are your impact. This is your unique value-add.

Even recent graduates can show impact and value-add. Were you able to answer any of the above questions related to:

- Joining a club or association
- Holding after or during-school jobs
- Contributing to a project
- Being elected to a position

I've named another very helpful tool the So What Tool. This blunt tool will help you find the impact of an action.

To use the So What Tool, find any action statement on your resume:

"I fixed...."

"I solved...."

"I partnered...."

"I developed...."

"I increased...."

Read that action statement out loud. Then ask yourself, *So what? Who cares? Why does this matter to the company?*

For example, you would read out loud: "Used Excel to create spreadsheets for the Production Department." And then you would ask yourself, *So what if I used Excel for them? Who cares about this? Why does this matter to the hiring company?*

If you have an answer to *So What? Why does this matter?* it means that you made something better, and that is further proof that you deserve the job instead of someone else. If you don't have an answer, don't worry; just leave the statement there. The action statement shows that you can do the job. The result proves that you deserve the job.

Do you see the difference?

You're striving for as many impact/results statements as possible because they are your proof.

You will not be able to answer every question for every position in your Experience section, but the list and the So What Tool will give you good food for thought. I'll bet that by asking yourself these questions after every statement, you'll come up with more details and juicier information than you ever thought possible.

By the way, volunteer jobs count. Recruiters see volunteer positions as legit as paid positions. If you have volunteered at an organization in your field, that makes you look focused and very committed to that field.

And, as previously mentioned, clubs count. Holding a club position shows you possess natural leadership skills in an area you're interested in. Your help with club fundraising, particularly if you organized or led the effort, is impressive. If you helped raise more money than in previous years, that is an impact statement. If you improved something, anything, at the club, even if you only improved it a little, then you can state that impact.

Part 2: State How You Created the Impact

The formula is incredibly easy: [Impact] by [action that created the impact]. Here are some examples:

- Increased sales revenue 30% by hiring more regional sales managers.
- Reduced employee turnover 10% by negotiating better benefits terms with the company insurance broker.
- Enhanced employee and executive relations by establishing annual meetings, including hosting smaller Q&A panels.
- Reduced equipment theft by establishing exit interviews.

It's really that simple. There are no acronyms to remember and no writing out a story until you get it right. State the impact clearly, and then state how you created the impact. You don't need more than that to show value on your resume and LinkedIn profile. The simpler the statement, and the more you use statistics, metrics, numbers, percentages, estimates, etc., the more powerful the statement.

It's important to note that impact statements can result from hard (technical) and soft skills. Notice in that list of questions that I did not divide the questions into hard and soft skills and didn't label them that way. That's because you want ALL skills to have an impact on your resume and your LinkedIn profile.

Don't worry if you struggle with impact. Everyone does. Even my top 1% of executive clients have trouble demonstrating impact, so you are not alone.

One client, Gerard, couldn't tell me anything about his successes. Now, I could tell from his resume that Gerard had impact to talk about because he had been hired to oversee the finances of one division. When he said the company appointed him to lead two more divisions, I knew he was an expert. But when I asked him specific questions about his improvements to the company, he simply said, "Soozy, this is complicated. I worked really hard."

No doubt he did. But if you can't articulate your impact to me, your ardent supporter, how will you articulate it to the hiring manager, who sees you as Candidate #43?

Here's an example of a conversation with a client about impact:

Me: I see on your resume that you used Excel. How did you use it?

Client: To create spreadsheets.

Me: Okay, what were the spreadsheets for?

Client: So, the bosses could see the overall monthly activities.

Me: While inputting information into Excel, did you notice anything that could be done better?

Client: Oh, yes. They were giving me the information as it came in, so piecemeal. So, then I started doing weekly reports before the monthly report so I could see every week if anything changed before the month ended.

Me: And how did that help you?

Client: It made life easier for me because it saved me time. Also, the reports were more accurate, and I could point out specific points of change, good and bad. So, I would give them the report with a side note summarizing the changes I saw.

Me: Interesting. And how did that help them?

Client: They discovered sooner where they were saving money and where they were wasting money.

Me: Do you know how much money they saved as a result of this?

Client: About $100K this year.

Me: That's amazing! Why isn't that on your resume?

Client: I don't know. I didn't think it was important.

The client didn't understand the importance of impact and how to use it on her resume. I know you can figure this out. Just follow my steps above. As I said, even if it's a slight improvement, you made something better, and now you have a simple and effective way to demonstrate it.

Every improvement counts, even if it was tiny and only you noticed. It doesn't matter if you didn't get honored; it doesn't matter if your boss didn't see it; it doesn't matter that nobody complimented you. You can use that impact as long as you witnessed the improvement and speak about how you made that improvement happen. That improvement is proof that you deserve the job instead of someone else. Skills and actions are not enough proof.

STEP 2:

ADDRESS THE COMPANY'S NEEDS

The Problem: How to Make the Hiring Team Notice You

Addressing the company's needs is the second most important thing you will do in your resume. Period.

As you know, you have competition for every job that you apply to. I've been both a recruiter and an executive career advisor. As a recruiter on the hiring side of the desk, all the resumes looked alike to me. That's because the resumes all said the same thing. All candidates in the same field send resumes with the same skillset and unhelpful word descriptors from the Terms Not To Use list.

After reading these exact words on 150, 500, or 5,000 resumes, the hiring team gets bored and looks for a kernel—anything—of differentiation. If that differentiation is not apparent, but the resume contains all the skills and experience required to do the job, it goes in the "maybe" pile.

That "maybe" pile grows into hundreds of candidates who can possibly do the job. Recruiters have to choose a certain number of people to interview per day; otherwise, they'd be interviewing all day, and it's cumbersome. Most resumes are so tedious to read that the "maybe" pile of candidates quickly gets higher.

In all this tedium and chaos, how do *you* get noticed?

Applicant Tracking System (ATS)

Your resume has to get through the company's first line of defense: its applicant tracking system (ATS) or filtering software. This software comes in many shapes and sizes, and many companies make them.

The basic idea of the ATS software is to help recruiters and hiring teams filter out inappropriate and unqualified candidates. As annoying as this part is to job seekers, trust me when I tell you that the company needs this software. The hiring team receives five to thousands of resumes daily, and most of those resumes are wrong for the job.

In fact, I would venture that up to 98% of resumes are wrong for any job opening.

Some recruiters rely on the ATS software to reduce the queue of candidates, or at least prioritize the applications, and some recruiters look at every resume that comes in. The hiring company that uses the ATS does it so that the hiring manager doesn't have to make the hiring team look at Every. Single. Resume.

Instead, hiring teams can use this ATS software to search for resumes with the skills and experience required for the job. For more details on the ATS, go to "Make the ATS Work for You" in the Tips & Hacks Chapter at the end of this book.

Are these systems helpful? Absolutely.

Are they flawed? Absolutely.

However, the alternative of looking at every single resume is sometimes just not doable.

So, count on your resume having to get past the awkward ATS before a person can see it. That's just the way the world works now.

MYTHS

- There are "ATS-friendly" resume templates that ensure you get through to the hiring team.
- You can predict ATS searches by doing company research.
- AI resume review programs give you all the information and feedback you need to land an interview.
- Sending one version of the resume to multiple companies is just as effective as tailoring the resume to each position.
- AI programs are so advanced that your AI-based resume will represent you well to the hiring team.
- AI programs are so advanced that the hiring teams can't tell the difference between your writing and AI writing.
- Uploading the job description and your resume into an AI program ensures your resume will show the company that you have the skills to do the job.
- You can or should omit some crucial information on your resume so you have something to talk about during the interview.
- Hiring managers at companies in your field understand all of your statements in your resume because they work in your field. There is no need to clarify anything.
- The title of the job says everything about what the company needs.

The Solution: Address the Company's Needs in Your Resume

The solution to making the hiring team notice you is to add a title, summary, and skills section to your resume that specifically addresses the company's needs.

Part 1: Read the Job Description

Read the job description from top to bottom. That's right, every single word. Sometimes, important information and essential skills are mentioned in the last sentence, as if they're testing you to see if you read the whole description.

Do not just go by the title. This is a big mistake that many people make. It's easy to stick a generic title (e.g., Marketing, Operations, Law Professional) at the top. However, a manufacturing associate at a toy factory in Utah will differ greatly from a manufacturing associate at a beauty chain in Florida. They're going to have different skill requirements and different needs.

After reading the job description from top to bottom, match the skills, tools, and experience at least 60%. Some clients print out the job description and highlight the key skills and industry phrases they want to add to their resumes.

This matching is where men and women often differ. Men will apply to positions they are not qualified for or barely qualified for, while women will avoid applying to positions even if they are 100% qualified or overqualified.

Everyone should apply for positions for which they are at least 60% qualified. The remaining 40% should be used for learning (career advancement) and for words or phrases you don't know or aren't sure about.

If you match the position in skills, tools, and experience, you want to also ensure you like the job description. Don't apply for a position if you don't love how the company describes itself in the job posting. Does the company seem too liberal? Does the company seem too conservative? Does something seem off? Is it not trendy enough for you?

Just because you *can* do a job doesn't mean you should or want to do it.

Some job descriptions are very detailed, and some are very vague. The good news about vague job descriptions is you can add whatever you want to in the skills section. The bad news is that a vague job description gives you no idea what each hiring team member will search for. So, even with all your listed skills, you might be wrong and ignored.

If you apply to a job you might not want and land an interview anyway, that probably won't end well. Even though you can do the job, I guarantee that somewhere in the hiring process, your feelings of not loving the job will show up in your voice, body language, and interview answers. The interview process will not end well, and you will have wasted your and the interviewer's time.

By reading the entire job description and ensuring that you match and like the job, you will reject a lot of jobs. That is a scary feeling. That does not feel good at first. Bulk applications feel so much easier and less stressful. If you send 500 resumes, someone somewhere has to notice you, right?

Nope.

The Quick Apply option in apps like LinkedIn and Glassdoor is among the worst job search inventions ever. When you apply in bulk using the Quick Apply button on LinkedIn, you have the option to send the same resume to each position. I'm sure you've seen a few job postings, so do you think one resume fits all jobs? Of course not.

Applying for jobs is not like sales. You don't want a sales ratio here. Applying for 500 jobs and landing 50 interviews is not smart, it's desperate.

One IT executive, Sam, was doing just that, and he was feeling very lost and rejected. Who wouldn't? That many rejections are way too depressing and stressful. As soon as Sam learned a more focused, timesaving job search strategy, he went from zero interviews to six per week.

You might think, *But it takes so much time to edit my resume for each position!*

Not if you're picky about job applications. If you are selective about the jobs you apply for, then you will apply for fewer jobs and have more time to spend on better job applications, and you will hear back more often from companies. It only takes a few more minutes to focus on the title, summary, and skills section in the top sections of the resume. Those few minutes are time well spent.

To give yourself more time and space for better applications, I want you to reject up to 90% of jobs. That's right, up to 90%.

When my clients hear this high rejection percentage, they get nervous. That's a lot of rejected jobs! And I know that rejecting the jobs will feel very uncomfortable after passing on 5, 6, 7 jobs. I know they will curse my name after they have let these jobs go by. And I say to them, curse away! Because what happens is the 8th or 9th or 10th job comes along, and it's perfect. You will be thrilled and willing to spend the extra time on that perfect job application because you will have the time, space, and mental energy for it. If you had applied to the other five to seven jobs, you would have wasted your time, and you might not want to take the time for the job that is worth your time.

The more you say *No* to inappropriate positions because you don't match them and you don't like them, the fewer rejections you will receive and the more time, space, and mental energy you will have to focus on matching the top sections (title, summary, and skills) of your resume to the positions that are right for you. You will get more responses for better jobs. You will see better ROI for your time and actions.

Rejecting jobs feels uncomfortable and lousy when you don't have a job, are on limited severance, or are running out of money. But I guarantee you that you will feel more empowered and less stressed when you say no than if you apply for every job.

Rejection emails come quickly, and recruiters sometimes ghost unqualified candidates. Some rejections happen within seconds because your resume didn't include a skill, or the application included some knock-out questions to determine who is truly qualified, but you weren't. Recruiters ghost candidates because they don't have enough time in the day to respond to everyone, especially people applying from a completely different field. Rejection is depressing, stressful, and frustrating. Let's reduce that.

Part 2: Match the Job Description

After reviewing the entire job description, if you determine you match the job and you like the job, you will move specific information from the job description to the top sections of the resume only: the title, the summary, and the skills section. So, yes, you're going to plagiarize the title, part of the summary, and the skills section on your resume directly from that awesome job description.

Let's start with the title because it's the first thing (after your name) the recruiter and the hiring team will see after you get through the ATS.

Figure 1 - Your Title

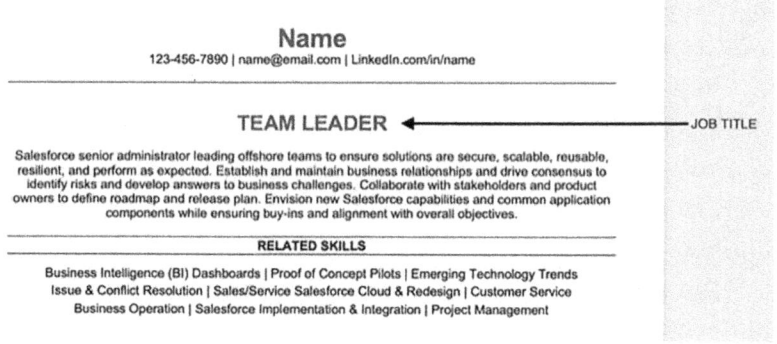

The Title

If you don't have a title at the top of your resume, add one. Add the title where I have shown you in Figure 1 above.

Use this QR code to see this image up close.

The title goes right below your contact information. Make the title of the job you're applying for. If the job is Assistant General Manager, you put Assistant General Manager at the top of your resume. If the job is Budget  Associate, put Budget Associate at the top. Don't make the title what you think it should be. Don't make the title what you want it to be. Don't make the title what you think you deserve to be called. You have no opinion here.

You have only two options: Apply to the job or don't.

Put the title exactly how the job posting has it. Plan on editing and changing this title for every application. This won't be too cumbersome because you've already followed Part 1, so you're only doing this a few times per week.

Job titles vary widely from company to company, division to division, and even team to team within one company. What is considered a Director in one place can be an Associate in another, and that isn't even based on company size; it is determined by how that specific company is structured. Sometimes, there is no structure, and leaders make up titles. Sometimes, leadership will create a whole new job and job title because you impressed them so much. If you come across a fantastic job description but you don't like the title, I recommend you use their title, anyway. The job description is infinitely more important than the title.

This also means you will never use the word Professional or Experienced in your title. Never. "Banking Professional," "Experienced Accounting Professional," or "Marketing Professional." You will never see a job description with the word Professional in the title. Ever.

When my daughter was looking for a part-time job while attending college in New York City, she sent her resume to dozens of places, and nobody responded. She got very frustrated and finally asked her mom for advice. She emailed her resume to me, and I added a title and told her to change the title every time for every job. Suddenly, she was getting calls for interviews. Yes, the title is that important.

Eye scans and surveys prove that the title is among the first things hiring people see when they open the resume. The title is your first impression because it's at the top, centered, and usually in bold, all caps, or both. And because it's the title of the position, the hiring team sees that, and you have made a great first impression.

Think of how attractive and engaging you look when the company's job title is at the top of the resume, and it's the first thing they see. Then, think how off-putting your resume looks if the title is slightly different than the position's title. You will look like you missed the mark. Putting the company's title at the top says that you understand the position and that the resume will prove why you're the best person for the job.

Your Summary

If you don't have a summary below the title, add one. Figure 2 below demonstrates where the summary goes.

Figure 2 - Your Summary

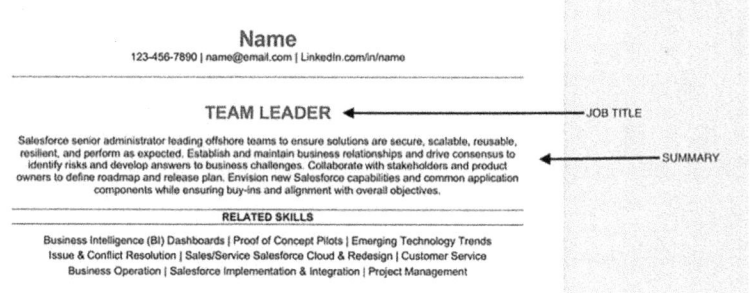

Use this QR code to see this image up  close.

The summary should not be about you. Many people, including my colleagues, use the summary as a career overview. But then you will look like everyone else. If you want to stand out and engage the hiring team, write a series of statements about how you help companies based on what the company needs, as outlined in the job description.

The company has laid out its needs in the job description. Use that information to make your case.

As mentioned previously, many people like to start the summary using adjectives such as "experienced," "passionate," and "successful." No, no, and no. "Innovative," "transformational," and "creative." No, no, and no.

Remember that rejection list? Reject those words because everyone uses them, so they are stale, and those adjectives are challenging to prove.

Self-descriptors are not reliable. Take the word "passion," for example. People use this very popular word to prove why they deserve the job. I could say that I'm the most passionate banana peeler in the world, but it doesn't mean it's true because I don't know about other banana peelers in the world or their passion. And how do I prove that passion?

The company isn't interested in your passion, experience, success, innovation, transformation, or creativity unless you can prove how those elements meet the company's needs and make the company better.

During my first interview for a magazine job right out of college, I told the interviewer, my future boss, that I was passionate about the work because several family members had worked in publishing for decades. My father was the Chief Financial Officer for St. Martin's Press—publishing is in my blood. Of course, I am passionate! My boss's response? "Good for you because we have long hours here. I hope your passion lasts!"

Instead of guessing at the right words to use or making up your own words and trying to convince the company that you're awesome, read the job description to understand the objectives and problems important to the company. Do they need help with organizing something? Do they need business development? Sales? Do they need someone to take on special projects?

Whatever they need, write a resume summary about your ability to do that. As in: Been there, done that. Even if it's only through volunteer or club work.

Here are examples of engaging summary first statements:

- Marketing specialist using digital tools to run social media campaigns and update the company website.
- Financial specialist reviewing spreadsheets and conducting informal audits to ensure best practices and optimal revenue.
- Proofreader, editor, and overall editorial support reviewing specific content to ensure error-free material optimized for websites, social media, and blogs.

Notice that none of these statements are about the applicant. They are all about the applicant meeting the needs of the company.

The only exception to the non-descriptor rule is "award-winning." If you won an award or more than one, even if the award is specific to a company or you were a team member who won an award, as long as the award(s) is related to your business, start your summary with "Award-winning...."

Using adjectives in the summary is so popular and unhelpful that I encourage you to read more about it in "The Challenge of Adjectives" in the Common Resume Mistakes Chapter.

Your Skills

In this section, I want you to plagiarize the heck out of the job description. If you don't have a skills section at the top of your resume, you should add one:

Figure 3 - Your Skills

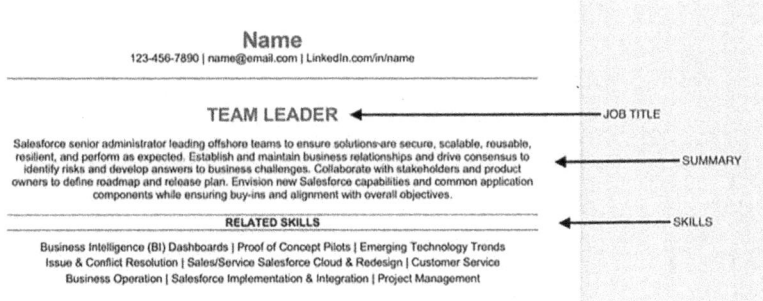

Figure 3 above shows where the skills section goes on your resume.

Use this QR code to see this image up close.

You can use a section divider like the one in the graphic above or simply label the section in bold, caps, or both. You can call it

CORE COMPETENCIES, PROFESSIONAL SKILLS, KEY SKILLS, or INDUSTRY SKILLS. I like RELATED SKILLS.

You have read the job description from top to bottom and determined what the company needs from you (title and summary). Now, you will show them you have experience with the tools they want you to use.

The skills section is a key part of your resume and is where many of my clients falter. I see perfectly qualified candidates miss exceptional opportunities every day because they didn't abide by the job posting for the skills section. The skills section is at the top so that recruiters and hiring teams can quickly assess whether you are a viable candidate. The exactness required for this section causes a lot of frustration and anxiety for job seekers. So many times, I have heard clients say, "I am qualified for this job! What do they want from me? How do I know what to add?"

The answer is *always* in the job posting. Use the job posting as your cheat sheet. If the job application was a test, the job posting has all your answers.

As you read every word of the job postings, you will see similarities and differences among job descriptions. For example, if you want to be an editor, you'll see that a lot of editorial jobs want similar skills from you, like impeccable grammar, word choice, and business writing. However, each company might go about its business differently. One company might need Google Docs. One might use Teams. One might use Slack. One company might want you to write all the editorial content for everything. One company might only want you to proofread the blogs and website content the writers put out.

Every time you use your resume to apply for a position, your skills section should reflect the specific skills and tools the job requires. Also, pay attention to the secondary Requested and Nice to Have skills that are sometimes posted. As you did with the title, plan on editing this skills section for each job application. After reading (and rejecting!) a bunch of job postings, you see that they all need similar tasks done, but you will see differences in how they want this and say this.

Continuing with the editor position example, if the company wants proficiency in Google Docs and you have experience using Google Docs, then put Google Docs in the skills section. If they use Teams, don't put Google Docs, put Teams. In this example, Google Docs is not a helpful tool on your resume because the company has made it clear that they use Teams. So, Google Docs is the term that they might search for in the ATS and on LinkedIn. Changing out the skills might seem tedious and unnecessary, but I guarantee you that matching your word choices to the job description will mean the difference between landing an interview and being ignored.

Why?

That ATS that I talked about before is most companies' first defense. Someone on the hiring side is going into the ATS (or LinkedIn) and might search for specific words associated with the position. Or, the ATS is ranking or rating your resume compared to all the other resumes based on matching skills and experience. You want your resume to appear at the top of the ATS queue, not the bottom. The hiring team is more likely to choose someone at the top of the queue than the bottom.

Using another example, if they are looking for someone who has experience with the limitations of a budget, and they search for "Budget," and you have "Finance Management" in your skills section, that's a commendable skill, but you may never get to use it because they might not see you. They might have searched for "Budget" because knowledge of budget compliance was a skill in the job description. As far as the ATS search is concerned, you don't appear to have that skill because you put "Financial Management" instead.

It feels natural and is understandable to use words that are familiar to you. For example, if a job calls for "information integration," and you think that the company means "data integration," then your natural response might be to add "data integration" instead to your skills section. Because that's the term you use and because "data integration" sounds better to you. But if you put "data integration" in the skills section, and the job posting has "information integration," you might not get an interview because they searched for a specific phrase not on your resume. You'll probably feel frustrated. *(I deserved that job!)*

I've had some frustrated clients say, "Of course! I know that! I've been doing that!" When I look at their resume, I see they've been replacing words, and they didn't even realize it.

When my clients feel frustrated that they are not landing interviews, we meet on Zoom and compare the job posting to the resume they used to apply. I will point out keywords, skills, and tools that they either changed or omitted. Every time this happens, without fail, the reaction is: "Oh, you mean EXACTLY the same?" Yes, if you want this job, I mean *exactly the same.* That's what plagiarizing the skills means.

If you see an acronym (e.g., DoD, SaaS, DEI, POS), research and ensure you know what the acronym stands for.

Sometimes, acronyms are very company-specific. Sometimes, the company spells out the acronym in the job posting, which is helpful, but that's not always the case. Don't guess.

I once searched "POS" for what I thought was Point of Service and got, no joke, 20 possibilities. Years ago, I was working with an executive and guessed at a company acronym, but I was wrong. That client was not happy.

One client, Jennifer, a Human Resources executive, insisted on using "DEI" on her resume. Having made that acronym mistake, I asked her what DEI stood for. She thought I was nuts. "Diversity, Equity, and Inclusion!" she laughed. I told her that in the thousands of job posts I have seen and the thousands of resumes I've seen, I had never seen it written DEI. She insisted that it be written that way. I explained that if a company searches for DE&I, spells it out, or searches "diversity," she will miss out on opportunities.

If you don't know what an acronym stands for, leave it off your resume. You can then ask about it during the interview, and if you have experience with it, talk about it then.

STEP 3:

OPTIMIZE YOUR LINKEDIN PROFILE

The Problem: The Job Search Feels Slow

If you are actively job hunting, your LinkedIn profile must be engaging. Most LinkedIn profiles are not. They're boring. Ineffective. Useless.

What do I mean by boring, ineffective, and useless? I mean generic. Empty.

With over 1 billion users in over 220 countries, LinkedIn is challenging. Many profiles are empty, and some users aren't active. People post articles about non-business subjects like illness, food, and lost children. They also rant in long articles. Most people don't even know how to use all the features.

However, LinkedIn is the best global connector that we have. It is a source of jobs, but it is also a networking behemoth. It will serve you well if you can harness its power and connect with, search for, and talk to people. I've had many clients resist LinkedIn, and then when they saw its benefits, like finding a job sooner, they grew to like it. Get out your proverbial weed whacker and start whacking through the LinkedIn weeds.

Many people think the resume and the LinkedIn profile are the same, but they're not. They are two very different tools with different purposes. Your LinkedIn profile—your professional face to the world—is meant to attract attention in a way your resume cannot. For more information about this difference, go to the "Start Your Job Search on LinkedIn" in the Common Resume Mistakes section later in this book.

When you're ready to use LinkedIn, your profile has to be optimized. When you become active and interact with people (especially recruiters!), they will look at your profile, and you don't want it to be generic, empty, or useless.

Some of my clients initially feel quite uncomfortable with their new profiles. They feel better modeling their profiles after someone else who appears successful. Some clients have asked me, "Why don't we just put a job title at the top?" Or "I don't want to promote my awards." Or "I think we should just keep it simple."

While I understand this hesitation, the last thing you want is to look like everyone else in your field. The point of optimizing your LinkedIn profile is to stand out in searches, not hide. If you look like everyone else, you won't stand out and, therefore, you won't be contacted.

MYTHS

- Nobody gets a job on LinkedIn.
- LinkedIn is too big to be helpful.
- You will receive too much spam on LinkedIn for it to be useful.
- LinkedIn is the same as your resume.

The Solution: Optimize Your LinkedIn Profile

It is imperative that you optimize your Headline, About section, and Experience section with impact, impact, and more impact. You also want to pack your Skills section with industry keywords and phrases so that hiring teams find you in searches. Following are specific pointers for each area of your profile.

The LinkedIn Headline

For starters, don't use the LinkedIn headline default. LinkedIn's headline default is the first position listed in the Experience section. Most people do this.

For example, if you sell real estate, and your first or current position is with Soozy Miller Real Estate, the headline default will be Soozy Miller Real Estate. Awesome. Guess how many other real estate sellers there are? A lot. Guess how many real estate sellers will end up in a search for "real estate sales"? A lot. This is boring. Ineffective. Useless.

Figure 4 - Your Headline

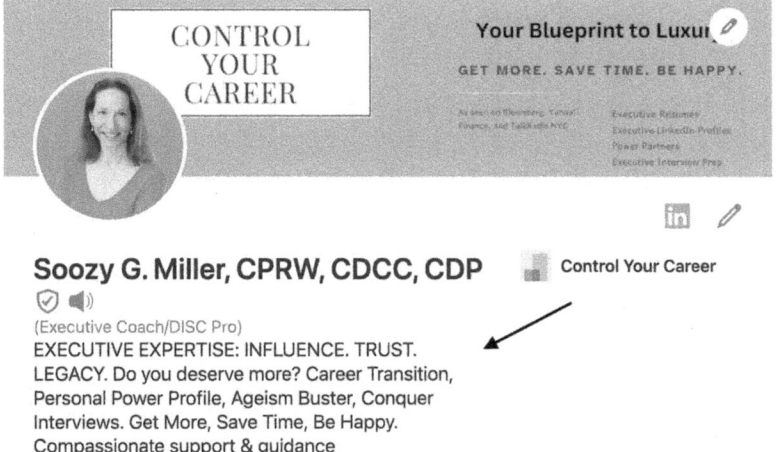

Review Step 1. Use your impact and value-add to create your headline.

See Figure 4 above for an example of where your headline goes.

Use this QR code to see this image up close.

You have up to 220 characters for your headline to show why someone or a company should choose you instead of someone else.

For a variety of reasons discussed earlier, Don't use the following terms:

- Passion
- Hard Working
- Innovation
- Transformation
- Successful [fill in the blank]
- Entrepreneur

These don't help anyone get to know you and your strengths. They are way too generic.

I want to point out that "innovation" and "transformation" are particularly troublesome. Not only are these overused terms, but they're usually not even true.

Everyone thinks (or hopes) that their work is innovative, but a deeper conversation will usually reveal that they are simply a creative problem solver. One client, Helen, claimed that she was innovative because she was the first person to gather fellow leadership into a room to discuss a long-standing problem, where others had failed to do this. While she gets kudos for this, that is not innovation; that's everyday problem-solving.

Helen was just more successful. So, she could speak to creative problem-solving as one of her strengths.

"Innovation" is a tricky word. It can only be defined in context. For example, the wheel could be thought of as innovative. Pre-sliced bread could be innovative. The latest update on an app could be innovative. Unless you can prove that your impact truly transformed the business as they know it and you helped the company do something or accomplish something truly new in the field, don't use "innovative."

The word "transformation" strikes fear at the heart of hiring teams because it assumes operations and systems overhaul, and that assumes IT headaches and big spending. Some job postings call for transformation. If not, you don't want to go there.

If you have some version of "innovation" and "transformation" in your job search materials, someone might ask about this, and they are very difficult to justify. What happens if you label something innovative, and then, during an interview, you discover that the hiring company did that three years ago? Or worse, they did that three years ago and lost a lot of money. Now, how innovative and transformational do you think you look to them? Better to just avoid these words.

To add impact, look at the impact statements that you wrote as a result of Step 1. If you have increased revenue, even as a volunteer or for a club, you can add that to the headline. It is even better if you have the numbers by which you increased revenue.

If you doubled revenue, you could put "2X Revenue" in your headline.

If you improved a process, you could put "Process Improvement" in your headline.

If you were given an impressive budget because of past wins, you could put "$[#] Budget."

If you have won any awards—any awards at all—put Award-Winning in the headline before your current title, like Award-Winning Publishing Assistant. It doesn't even matter if the award was related to the Publishing Assistant position. Put it there anyway.

You can put specific tools in your headline, but only if you're a true expert and you find that many companies you're applying to want that specific tool. One of my clients, Noelle, put 3X Salesforce Certified as part of her headline because she is a Salesforce expert and uses Salesforce constantly to help her customers. However, she also added leadership impact statements to her headline. As a result, she went from zero interest to several emails and phone calls every week.

Narrow each impact to one to three words and put a series of words in the headline until you reach the 220-character max. You can do this using individual impact phrases divided by a symbol:

> Award-Winning Publishing Geek | New Authors & Celebrity Icons | 10 NYT Bestsellers | 50 Influencers on Deck | Evangelize Through the Written Word

Or you can add statements as your title:

> Award-Winning Publishing Geek celebrating new authors & celebrity icons through books & the written word. 10 NYT Bestsellers & 50 Influencers on deck

That's about 170, not even the max, and there could be more keywords. But you get the specialty, and you get the impact.

The About Section

The About section is a bit more complex, so follow my lead. See Figure 5 below to reference the About section.

The About section on LinkedIn is about proving your headline. You have to put impact and value-added keywords in your headline, so now you want to demonstrate and detail them. Someone searched for your skills, and your headline came up in their search results. Now, the About section proves your unique value-add, strengths, and impact.

Figure 5 - Your About Section

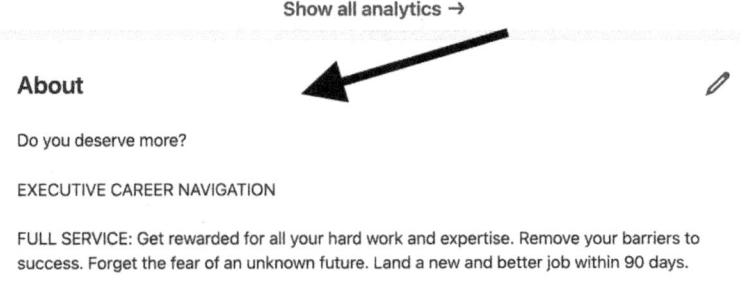

Show all analytics →

About

Do you deserve more?

EXECUTIVE CAREER NAVIGATION

FULL SERVICE: Get rewarded for all your hard work and expertise. Remove your barriers to success. Forget the fear of an unknown future. Land a new and better job within 90 days.

How would it feel if you could control your career within days? Do you deserve a better position at a better company with a salary bump? Do you want a situation that feeds your soul?

If you have the expertise and background I can help you amplify your authentic authority. We will simply focus and reinforce your impact and strengths to ensure that you have control over your own destiny.

Use this QR code to see this image up close.

You have up to 2,600 characters in the About section, which might seem like a lot, but when you're trying to show your impact and value-add, you'll see how quickly you run out of space.

Do not simply add skills to the About section. As I said earlier, you can add one or two skills in the headline IF you are an expert and use those skills to create impact. Don't add a list of skills to the About section if the section seems short. That will not make you stand out; it will make you look like everyone else in your field because, as stated before, everyone else has the same skills. You already have a skills section in your LinkedIn profile, and having juicy keywords in that skills section will get you found in searches.

There are various formulas and suggestions out there for writing the About section. In advising hundreds and hundreds of people through this and observing the results, here is my very easy and impactful formula.

Your first paragraph should contain your Why statement. Why do you do what you do? Why does your specialty matter? Why is your work important to your clients and customers? Remember, don't use communication, passion, innovation, leadership, or transformation to prove your point. This is not only about making money, even if you are in sales, and increasing revenue is your strength. In this first paragraph, state why you are doing what you do. Then, you demonstrate this Why with an example of your impact. Pick an impact statement from your resume that exemplifies how your Why made a company, client, project, or process better.

The About section's first two to three lines are the most crucial. They hook the reader. When your profile lands in someone's LinkedIn search results, and they click on your headline, your profile comes up with the first two to three lines of the About section. The visitor must click "see more" to get more information. See Figure 6 below, which references the "see more" option.

Figure 6 - Your About Section "See More"

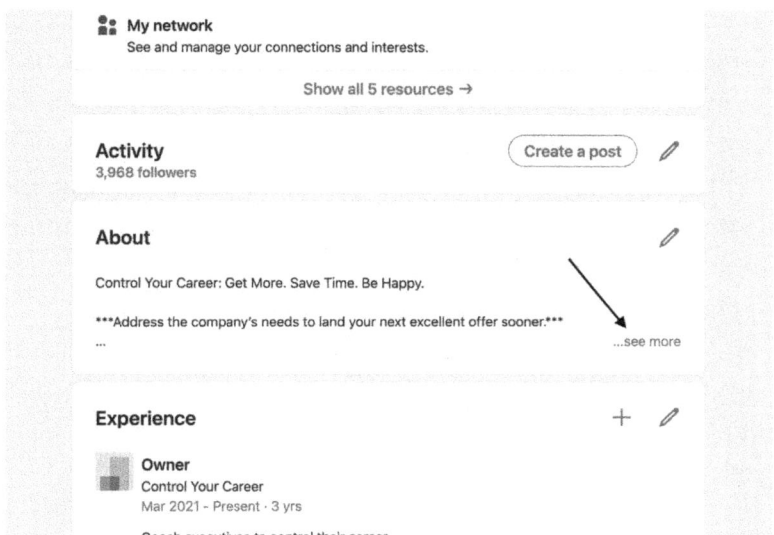

You want them to click that button.

Use this QR code to see the image up close.

Your second paragraph will be a hybrid formula. You will start with "I am particularly proud of:" and then state three of your favorite impact statements and why you are so proud of each one. Take your three favorite impact statements straight from the Experience section of your resume, and for each one, explain why you are so proud of that accomplishment.

Admittedly, this content may not max out your 2,600 characters. Don't worry about that; just concentrate on details and proof of your experience/expertise.

Skills

The skills section of your LinkedIn page is crucial for your profile landing in search results. Recruiters, headhunters, and hiring managers are on LinkedIn every day, multiple times a day, looking for people with specific skills to fill positions.

You have up to 100 entries for skills. That's not characters, that's not words, that's entries. "Business Development" is one entry. "Advanced Excel" is one entry. "Diversity, Equity & Inclusion" is one entry. So is "DEI."

Max out the skills section and get as close to 100 entries as possible. LinkedIn will offer suggestions as you enter skills into the box, and you can use those suggestions and make up your own.

Also, because you have read Step 2, you have read a lot of job postings, and you've seen the variety of skills companies look for in your field. As you reject job postings, you can still add their skills and keywords to the skills section on LinkedIn. As explained previously, companies have myriad ways of saying the same thing. Remember the reference to Google Docs, Teams, and Slack? Well, the LinkedIn skills section is where you can put all three! Even if your most recent resume has Google Docs because of a specific job application, you can still put Teams and Slack in your LinkedIn skills section, and another company will find you for another position.

LinkedIn might be the prevalent job board, but it is not the only one. See more about other job boards in the Common Resume Mistakes section at the end.

STEP 4:

CONQUER EVERY INTERVIEW

The Problem: Interviews Are Nerve-Racking and Stressful

You applied for a job by sending in your resume, which you filled with impact statements and focused the top sections on the company's needs, so now you have an interview.

The resume got you the interview, but now it's up to you to demonstrate in person (or video) that you're the best person for the job. And now, here comes pressure. Stress. Anxiety.

Often, whoever "wins" the interview wins the job. You can have a terrible or a great resume, but if the interviewer doesn't think you're a good fit for the position, you won't get the job.

You're probably thinking:

What if I answer a question wrong?

What happens if I don't understand a question? Will I look stupid?

What happens if they ask for my spirit animal, and I choose the wrong animal?

What if I forget what I'm supposed to say?

How do I know what the interviewer is going to ask me? How do I anticipate questions?

Let's reduce that stress, shall we?

First of all, don't anticipate the questions the interviewer will ask. You can't. You have no idea what they will ask. If you try to memorize entire scripts and the interviewer asks you something off-script, you will panic. The interviewer might see something on your resume that he/she thinks is particularly interesting that you never thought was important, and suddenly, you're answering questions and discussing a topic that you never expected.

The first interview will probably be with a recruiter, and that will be mostly about confirming that your skill set and experience match what they need. Also, the first interviewer might observe your energy level to determine if your energy matches what they expect for the position.

If you don't pass the first interview, consider that a good result. If they say, "No, thank you" during the conversation, they won't drag you along and make you wonder. Your skills weren't right, or your energy wasn't right. Either way, you probably dodged a bullet, even if you remember loving the job posting. Something didn't align, and at least you know that right away.

When you get past the first interview, the questions and conversation will be more about cultural fit as you move up the hiring chain. They have confirmed that you have the basic skills and background for the job, and now they want to get more specifics about your expertise and how you have used your skill set in the past. This is where your impact differentiates you and helps you.

When the interviewer asks the first question, "Tell me about yourself," 99% of job candidates (high school graduates to CEO) will talk about their education, passion, how long they have been in the business, and their skills.

When asked during interviews, "Why should we hire you?," 99% of job candidates (high school graduates to CEO) will talk about their passion, how long they have been in the business, and their skills.

When asked during interviews, "Why should we choose you instead of someone else?" 99% of job candidates (high school graduates to CEO) will talk about their passion, how long they have been in the business, and their skills.

 NO.

I'm telling you right now that those answers are interview suicide. You're done. You're over. Next candidate, please.

Or, even worse, those answers encourage hiring team ghosting. Why?

The interviewer is asking these sometimes seemingly stupid and overly vague questions because they are trying to figure out why they should hire you, as opposed to someone else. Everyone before and after you answered the same way: education, passion, longevity, and job skills. So now the interviewer feels annoyed and doesn't know who to speak to next. If five people or 1,000 people give the same answer, how do you choose who to hire? Their "maybe" pile is growing by the minute, so they will take a beat and figure out where to put their time and who deserves a follow-up. That "beat" is you waiting.

MYTHS

- All recruiters are experienced in the field for which they are hiring.
- A bad interview means that you don't get the job.
- Being unable to answer some questions automatically means you don't get the job.
- A great interview conversation means you will be recommended for the next step.
- Pausing to think of an answer makes you look incompetent.
- Asking for clarification about something in the job posting makes you look stupid or desperate.

The Solution: Know the Company's Needs and Goals

Know what the company needs and its goals, and use your impact to address them. Treat the company as the hero in their field.

To conquer any interview and impress the hiring team, make it very clear how you can address their needs and make the company better.

I cannot stress this enough. So, I'm going to say it again: *To conquer any interview, make it very clear how you can address the company's needs and make the company better.*

The company wants to hire someone to fix a problem or to help them accomplish something. That information is in the job description. If you want to be their next hire, demonstrate how your impact can fix their problem or help them meet that goal, and prove it by showing how this action made a past company better.

Like I said, going into the interview, you already kind of know the company's needs and culture, so go to your resume summary and go to your Experience impact statements and see where you have addressed this sort of problem before and made the company better.

The best way to prepare for an interview—every interview every time—is to read the job description repeatedly and visit the company's website to see their mission, so that you know what they want for the position and are more familiar with their culture.

Never take an interview on the spot. If someone from the company calls and asks for five minutes of your time, never say yes. Don't try to be spontaneous in the interview; this doesn't work in your favor. Tell them you are busy (even if you aren't) and reschedule for another time, even if that's in one hour.

You're doing this because you want to be prepared for every interview, whether it's the first interview or the fifteenth interview.

Remember, in Step 2, we covered reading the job posting from top to bottom and deciding if you like the position or if you match it. Because you've read the job posting completely before heading to the interview, you already have an idea of their culture. You know if the culture is going to be more liberal or more conservative. You have an idea of what the company does in the world.

Take the time before the interview to look at the job posting again. Even if you've reviewed it six times before, read it again to ensure you understand the company's pain points, needs, objectives, mission, and challenges. Then look at your Experience section in your resume and pick one or two impact statements—not skills, not actions—impact statements that demonstrate that you have addressed this issue before *and* made the company better. Don't plan to read these points like a script, but keep the ideas handy for the interview.

After you have reviewed the job posting and figured out which impact statements address the company's needs, you'll want to fill out this form:

> I saw in your job posting that you need [issue here*]. My name is [your name]. I have extensive experience in [industry or field]. My most recent job was with [company name] where I [state accomplishment]. Prior to that I worked at [previous company name] where I [state accomplishment]. My areas of expertise include [skills].

*Note: The issue is not the need to fill the position; it's the issue that the company needs the person in that position to address.

My esteemed colleague, Joe Stimac, created this template for his website interviewready.com. Joe has been helping Fortune 50 companies and the Department of Defense interview and hire for decades.

This is a great template and foundation for answering the dreaded questions: "Tell me about yourself," and "Why should we hire you instead of someone else?"

Notice that the questions are about you: "Tell me about *you*. Why should we hire *you*?" So, you should talk about yourself, right? Not so fast.

With the questions, "Tell me about yourself," and "Why should we hire you instead of someone else?" the interviewer is asking about you, yes, but the questions are simply a bad way of finding out how you will help them. The interviewer is not trying to trick you; many interviewers are bad at interviewing and simply don't know how to get the information they need from you to determine if they should hire you. "Tell me about yourself" is an ineffective and awkward way of asking you to prove yourself.

After you've completed the template, make a list of questions about the company and the job. If something seems funny in the job description, note it and plan to ask about it. If something resonates with you, plan to ask about it. Ask about something unclear in the job posting (e.g., an acronym not spelled out). The more you know, the better you can address their needs. The best interviews are conversations, not interrogations. Chances are the interviewer didn't write the job description, so your question might spark an interesting conversation. You won't look stupid with these questions; you will look interested and engaged.

But you can't ask something like, "What's the company culture like?" or "How's the communication here?" because those are too general, so the interviewer will probably only give an extremely and unrealistically positive answer.

By asking more specific questions, you will get helpful information and have more ammunition for answers. The more information you have about the company, employees, leadership, culture, gaps, issues, and priorities, the better you can address that and talk about how you will improve their lives and help them achieve their outcomes faster.

Questions You Can Ask

Some examples of helpful questions you can ask are:

Where did my predecessor fail? What do I have to follow up on?

What does success look like at 30, 60, and 90 days? How is this measured?

What are your top three priorities for this job?

What deadlines should I know about?

What complications or barriers might I encounter as I try to achieve goals or fix problems?

What does promotion look like? Is it entirely based on merit, or must I wait a prescribed amount of time?

How difficult is it to get things done here? If I see a problem, can I fix it, or do I need to go through a rigorous approval process before I can touch anything?

When you have more information, your answers will be more helpful to the company.

Here is an example of conquering a vague question during an interview:

Interviewer: Tell me about yourself.

You: Well, I see in the job posting that you're looking for someone to help with [issue here]. I have extensive experience in [industry or field]. My recent job was with [job title], where I [state impact]. Before that, I worked at [company name], where I [state impact]. My areas of expertise include [state areas].

Interviewer: That sounds good. That's what we need.

Here is another more complicated sample:

Interviewer: Tell me about yourself.

You: I am persuasive. At Soozy Miller Real Estate, I helped the salespeople expand their territory by cold calling prospects outside their territory and explaining the benefits of our sales process. More people agreed to a meeting than we expected, and soon, our agents had regular meetings, and we sold more houses.

Interviewer: That sounds good. That's what we need.

The second sample is more complicated because you notice that I suggested you use an adjective: persuasive. Up to now, I have told you to avoid adjectives on your resume and LinkedIn profile. For interviews, adjectives can work. Let me explain.

First, you'll notice that I didn't use any words from the banned list:

- Passion
- Hard Working
- Innovation
- Transformation
- Successful [fill in the blank]
- Entrepreneur

That's important, and I still stick to this rejection list. And I stick by avoiding adjectives in your resume and LinkedIn profile, unless you have impact proof.

But an interview is different. When you're asked a question in an interview like, "Tell me about yourself," especially if it's the very first question, you want to talk about yourself in a way that is helpful and true. Do so in a way that you can prove and is helpful to the company.

How do you do this? Look at your impact statements on your resume as a result of doing Step 1. I'm absolutely positive that you can come up with more descriptive adjectives than the banned list to describe the impact. Use a Thesaurus if you want to.

Here is your template for creating the response:

I am [adjective]. When I was at [company], I [impact statement].

It's as simple as that. Have two or three examples of this handy for interviews and networking.

If you want to get down to more details, see the "The Challenge with Adjectives" in the Tips & Hacks Chapter.

Change is uncomfortable, and your interview habits probably feel comfortable. I understand it feels better now to continue answering interview questions with education, passion, longevity, and job skills. But I encourage you not to use these answers. They will not serve you. Not if you want the job.

This is so important and so under-used that I'm going to say it a third time: **For interviews, make it very clear how you can address the company's needs and make the company better.**

You may experience a bad interview or an inept interviewer during the hiring process. One IT executive client, Brad, asked the interviewer a technical question, and the interviewer had no idea what Brad was talking about. The interviewer immediately admitted that she did not know the IT world; she had just been hired to initially screen candidates. The hiring company probably went the cheap route and hired her for a lower contract fee because of this lack of experience. This happens all the time.

But really, anyone along the hiring chain could ask you an uncomfortable or ridiculous question. One company invited me to interview for an IT coaching position. The interviewer asked me which CMS (client management system) I use, and I told them Trello. Then they asked me to describe, step by step, the most difficult maneuver I've ever performed on Trello. *Huh?* What about the most difficult client? What about the most interesting client situation? That was a turnoff, and I didn't want to work for them.

When you get into an interview, and the interviewer comes off as weird, tired, inexperienced, or bored, you still have to hold your ground and prove why you deserve the job. Think of the company as the hero in your field. What will you do to support and lead the hero into conquering their goals? Focus on how you can help them. Think of the company, not yourself, and you will conquer all interviews.

STEP 5:

SHOW YOUR UNIQUE SOFT SKILLS

The Problem: Hard and Technical Skills Are Not Enough to Stand Out

Soft skills are challenging on a resume because people don't show them. Or, when people try to show them, they use general and unhelpful skills from the reject list. Or they think soft skills are personality traits, which they are not.

Every resume I've looked at in my 10 years of coaching, resume writing, and recruiting has contained the word "communication" or some form of "good communicator." Seriously, every single resume. To be fair, almost every job description I've seen includes the requirement for "excellent communication" or something similar.

We have discussed the reject list and the complications with using adjectives. A skill like "detail-oriented" is not necessarily important for every job.

If you feel you are a good communicator or a team player, that's great, but if everyone around you says they are good communicators, how do you prove you are? I'll get to that in a moment.

First, why do soft skills matter?

Here's an example. I helped a company recruit for some technical positions, and for each of the positions, the hiring manager required only one technical skill (one piece of software), and all the rest of the requirements were soft skills such as:

- Must be okay with peer review. This is a collaborative team, and we always try to find the best solutions for our customers.

- Must be able to lead small and large meetings and make everyone feel comfortable speaking their minds.

- Must be comfortable reaching out to all levels of personnel to maintain communication and ensure everyone has what they need.

See what I mean? All three of the above requirements are based on the ability to get along with others and communicate, which are soft skills. Hard/technical skills are often not the most important, by far.

And yet, 99% of resumes include only technical skills.

If you're applying for a marketing position, you want to show your marketing skills. But what makes you different if you're the 90th candidate and the last 89 candidates all had the same marketing skills? Your unique soft skills will get you noticed every time.

Consider this report that was re-printed in Harvard Business Review in March 2022[1]:

> *Research conducted by Harvard University, the Carnegie Foundation and Stanford Research Center has concluded that 85% of job success comes from having well-developed soft and people skills, and only 15% of job success comes from technical skills and knowledge.*
>
> *93% of employers believe soft skills are "very important" or "essential", while 97% say interpersonal skills are key to business growth and success. Further, 91% of organizations say they want more soft skills.*
>
> *Soft skills in the workplace enable organizations to effectively and efficiently use their technical skills and knowledge without being hampered by interpersonal issues, infighting, and poor public and market perceptions.*
>
> *SHRP reports that 46% of new employees fail within 18 months and that 89% fail because of a lack of soft skills. A lack of soft skills is often the reason that employees fail to perform at work.*

Ironically, this is a reprint from 1918! So, the importance of soft skills has been true for decades. The article might as well have been printed today.

---

[1] National Soft Skills published by the Harvard Business Review, March, 2022. Retrieved from https://www.nationalsoftskills.org/the-soft-skills-disconnect/ January 30, 2025.

As you move up the organizational ladder, soft skills become increasingly important. When you get to the manager level, the soft skills become known as leadership skills. Especially in the IT world, the difference between a worker bee and a manager is the soft skills. Do people trust you? Do you promote connection? Have you improved productivity? Do you learn from your mistakes? These are soft skills, and they are absolutely vital for career advancement.

MYTHS

◆ Soft skills are personality traits.

◆ Hard work, passion, and workplace longevity are soft skills.

◆ Interviewers know how to discuss your soft skills with you.

The Solution: Demonstrate Your Unique Skills

Demonstrate your unique and specific soft skills. Remember that list of questions from Step 1? Here they are again:

- How did I add/contribute to revenue?
- How did I improve a process or procedure?
- How did my work benefit a client? Make their life easier?
- How did my work save the company time and/or money?
- How did I develop/expand the business?
- How did I increase the customer base?
- How did I improve/enhance a project?
- How did I solve a problem?
- How did I enhance teamwork?

- How did I improve policy? Compliance?
- How did I influence someone to make a better decision?
- How did I use data or research to improve something or solve a problem?

This list of questions will help you determine your softer skills.

After reading Step 1, if you still want to say you're a good communicator, at least attempt to prove how your communications led to some company success.

After reading Step 1, if you still want to say you're a team player, try to prove how your teamwork impacted the organization.

After reading Step 1, if you still want to say that you're detail-oriented, make sure that the position calls for you to focus on details, in which case you want to prove how paying attention to details impacted the organization.

Without the proof (the impact), you're just another applicant saying that you're great at something, which may or may not be true and may or may not be important for the job.

There is an old expression: *You land the job with hard skills and keep the job with soft skills.* But there is so much competition now for any given job; let's try landing the job with soft skills and then keeping the job by using those soft skills.

For further information about the complication of adjectives, see "The Challenge of Adjectives" in the Tips & Hacks Chapter at the end of this book.

ABOUT AI

As of 2025, AI is rapidly gaining popularity since ChatGPT's beta version became public. People immediately started using AI to write general resumes, and recruiters started using AI to gather global contact lists. AI is being used on both sides of the hiring desk. The job search is becoming an AI vs. AI battle involving ridiculously high numbers.

Like the ATS, the quality of the AI program depends on the package. Some AI programs can 10X resume distribution in seconds due to the sheer number of people that these AI programs can immediately connect to. With a solid program, job seekers can find a job within two months, which is a very short time. Since 2020, the search can otherwise go on for years.

One AI recruiter firm I partner with uses a few AI programs to provide contacts, introductory emails, and even follow-up emails. They have developed excellent AI programs for contacting hiring managers, Human Resource executives, and other decision-makers related to hiring. This is quite impressive.

Another career agency that I worked with was a pure AI company. From client onboarding to job offers, they used four different AI programs, none of which were synced or compatible. So, whenever I worked with a client, I had one to four screens open. Out of seven clients, one landed a job.

Posting your one general resume to 500 applications through one-click applications probably won't get you noticed because the ATS or the knock-out questions will stop you. But sending your generic bad resume directly to thousands of contacts via AI, with some contacts bypassing the ATS, will get you noticed by at least a few people for very little effort, regardless of how bad your resume is. These distribution numbers are so high, and the outreach is so extensive that the rejections won't even matter. 500 rejections out of 10,000 direct emails is a no-brainer decision. The ratio is just too good.

Recruiters are charging thousands of dollars for this service, and it's worth the money if you only care about your immediate income and have no thoughts about your future career.

Challenges to AI

While AI sounds very appealing because it seems like a done-for-you-perfectly service, there are a couple of challenges here.

Challenge #1: Laziness. The ease of use and access to an enormous network immediately available with AI means that job seekers get lazy. My AI recruiter partners are swamped with clients because those clients distribute their sometimes bad (or mediocre) resumes to thousands of people.

Challenge #2: Waiting. You are not the only one doing this; therefore, you are one of many people flooding recruiters and the marketplace with your possibly bad general resume. This means you might not hear from the companies for a while because many people use a mass distribution system, and inboxes are flooded with (mostly inappropriate) resumes that hiring teams have to weed through. Understand that recruiters are using AI on their end as well to weed out hundreds or thousands of applicants. For more information, see "Make the ATS Work For You" in the Tips & Hacks Chapter.

Challenge #3: Some AI programs don't work. On the backend, behind the scenes, AI technology can be a mess. As the advisor, I see AI server issues, broken links, and vanishing emails. I have to get around all of this to provide excellent customer service.

If you use AI and send that one general resume to 10,000 people, I recommend being very confident about your interview skills. Because assuming that you get through the knock-out questions, the interview will be your next step. If you talk about your hard work, skills, loyalty, education, passion, communication, and leadership during the interview, you will have wasted the amazing opportunities AI provided.

Other versions of AI are automated resume search engine optimization (SEO) and keyword programs like Jobscan and Resume Worded, which can be used as part of your overall job search toolkit. Please be careful about relying too heavily on them because they are computer systems. While they are helpful, they also have limitations you should consider.

First, optimal resume writing is not automated or based on computer systems, at least not entirely. When you apply to a position through a job board, as we have covered, your resume will go through an applicant tracking system (ATS), but your resume also has to engage the people who see it after it passes through the software. So you have to satisfy the computer systems first and then the people. The programs are built to scan, recognize, and flag commanded words or parameters.

After the software scan, people became more interested in the human part, personality, and explanations of experience.

Second, automated tools are limited in scope and, therefore, don't know how to compute or categorize soft skills like solving problems and influencing decisions. The closest that any AI tool gets to softer skills is using words like "communication," "teamwork," and "analyst" (or "analytics"), all of which are much too vague and general to be helpful.

Job searchers' biggest mistake is using automated programs to create one resume to apply to all positions. While this may seem like the most straightforward route because it requires the least effort, it takes longer to find a job this way, let alone an appropriate job. Many of my clients have come to me after depending solely on an automated resume review program, sending out that one AI-based resume hundreds of times and hearing nothing. That doesn't surprise me at all.

Using only automated resume review tools without researching the hiring company and reading the job posting can cause unnecessary headaches.

For example, one of my clients, Catherine, a graphic designer, used Jobscan to compare her resume to a job posting, and Jobscan rated her resume as a 95% match. But she did not land an interview. When we compared the resume to the job posting, I saw that her resume did not include five of the six basic skills required for the job. I questioned the 95% compatibility rating, so we reviewed Jobscan's report. Jobscan had checked off every single one of those six skills on her resume, even though I could see they were not.

I've tested Jobscan so I can advise my clients appropriately. It told me to add "communication" to my resume, which I know is too general. I know recruiters would never search for that word—even for a communications leadership position. However, it is appropriate if you want to send out one generic resume to 150 companies.

Resume Worded assessed that I specialize in communication and marketing. Again, it is way too general, and the marketing is inaccurate.

Possibly, automated systems are more helpful for corporate positions. I specialize in writing executive resumes, consulting, and advising, so maybe the programs didn't know how to handle my communications experience.

I know one or two people who have relied solely on these systems and successfully landed an interview. They do work. Joel, an IT specialist, raved about how Jobscan helped him land his next job. A marketing assistant, Priscilla, also used Jobscan to land her next role.

But at least part of the challenge is that automated systems only know how to look for hard and technical skills because how do you search for behavior skills? Computer systems can't quantify or qualify human behavior, such as how you inspired a team out of a financial rut. Hence, they use unhelpful terms like "communication" because that's the closest to a soft skill these programs understand. These AI systems cannot be programmed to search for softer skills like: How do you solve problems? How do you work with teams? How do you influence decisions? How do you deal with compliance and rules? How do you monitor progress?

The crucial soft and leadership skills can make the difference between being rejected and being noticed, and automated systems can't get you there.

Everyone who does what you do has similar hard/technical skills. Therefore, putting only the automated system-suggested hard/technical skills on your resume will only get you partial success. You won't stand out. Your resume will go through the ATS and into the growing "maybe" pile because nothing on your resume says, *I am special.*

Use intelligent systems as one tool; don't rely entirely on them. In the hiring process, computer systems can only take you so far. In my experience testing various AI systems for resume writing, AI systems cause as many problems as they solve. And after a while, you need the human element.

As of 2024, companies in four U.S. states by law must provide the option for an AI review before applying for the job. How does this help or hurt you? See the "Make the ATS Work for You" section in the Tips & Hacks Chapter.

TIPS & HACKS

Common Myths

We've addressed some job search and resume myths. Let's add more (there are a lot!) and dig into more details on the ones we already covered because context is important. If you start with wrong notions, you will continue down that wrong path, and your job search will be more stressful, take longer, and be much more tedious. That won't help you.

Myth #1: A General Resume Works Well for Multiple Applications

One general resume might get you the next job, but it will not help you feel in control of your career. If you use one general resume to apply to all jobs, you will start again from scratch every time you have to search for a job.

Many people on social media (mainly LinkedIn) have claimed that they landed a job after 500 online job applications and three interviews. They think that this is a successful job search. It is not. 500 online applications and three interviews is a horrible ratio. This horrible ratio is because job seekers use one general resume for all online applications. As discussed in Step 2, most job seekers only read the job title. Also, most online applications have some version of a one-click apply option, so job seekers simply see a job title they like, click that one-click option, upload whatever resume is already there, and pray. And they're doing this hundreds of times per day or week.

The social media posters, who were ecstatic that they finally landed a job after throwing their resume everywhere (called Spray & Pray), claim they now have a successful formula for landing a job. Then thousands of people—yes, thousands—reply with grateful messages: "Thank you for the tip." "Thank you for the shortcut." "Thank you, I will try this." "God bless you; I finally have a way!"

NO.

See the "Make the ATS Work for You" section in the Tips & Hacks Chapter to explain why this tactic wastes time and energy.

I worked with one financial executive who had applied to 150 jobs the weekend before he hired me. Not surprisingly, he heard from zero. After we worked together, he got a job offer within a few days based on his new LinkedIn profile.

If you want to feel more in control of your job search, a more productive ratio is five applications max per week and up to five interviews within a few weeks. If you're not getting that kind of response, you are applying to the wrong jobs or not focusing the top parts of the resume to the company's needs. Or both. See Step 2.

Myth #2: A Resume Must Be One Page

I don't know where this came from, but it is wrong. And limiting! I've been an executive career advisor for more than 10 years, and only a few specific job openings have called for a one-page resume: a few Silicon Valley tech companies, Bloomberg, a few random Amazon departments, and a Long Island judge when he hired a clerk. That's it.

I know there have been articles on Forbes.com, themuse. com, and various career coaching blogs from celebrity career coaches suggesting a one-page resume. I also know entire Ivy League college career centers that suggest one-page resumes. Some career centers even mandate one page.

Most hiring teams are okay with up to two pages. There are a few problems with one-pagers. Follow my logic here.

If you're trying to fit your experience on one page, you won't have a title, summary, and skills section at the top. These top sections are crucial if you want the hiring team to notice you. Eye scans prove that recruiters and hiring teams notice the title first when they open a resume. Conversely, if you go the smart route and add a title, summary, and skills section at the top of your resume, you will barely have room for two jobs on that page.

If you want to fit the title, summary, skills, and your most recent jobs, you should reduce the type size to accommodate everything. But you don't want to go smaller than 10.5-point type for readability. I've seen 9-point resumes, which are not fun on the eyes.

When I'm done with my clients' resumes, even high school graduates, they have so much expertise and impact to demonstrate it's usually challenging to get the resume down to two pages. How could we possibly demonstrate their expertise on one page?

Many of my clients claim one page because their cousin's best friend's uncle used to hire people at his small company ten years ago. Save yourself wasted time and effort and go to controlyourcareer.net for help.

Myth #3: Your Resume Should Make You Feel Good About Yourself

Who would you prefer to like your resume: you or the hiring team? I'm going to guess the hiring team.

Of course, you should be proud of what you've accomplished, and you can be happy with your career choices. But the resume has not been written for you. Remember, in Step 2, we talked about the resume title? The title is not up to you because you want to put the company's job title, and your opinion doesn't matter. The resume title is a cold, unemotional marketing tool that makes your first impression and gets the reader interested in you because you've shown that you understand the position.

When I told one of my clients about the non-emotionality of the resume title, he responded, "That's okay. I have my wife to make me feel warm and fuzzy." Exactly! The resume is not the place for that feeling.

If you read Step 2, you know that the skills you put on your resume are not up to you, either. If you don't like using C++, and the job requires C++, then that job is not for you. Don't translate the skills into the language that you prefer. That doesn't work, and it won't get you interviews.

Myth #4: Tell Your Story in Your Resume

Many resume writers and coaches will tell you your resume is a story. I disagree. A story usually includes a beginning, a middle, and an end. An optimized resume has none of these. When you get to the interview, you can tell your career and impact stories, but the resume (and the LinkedIn profile) is not a story document.

The resume contains succinct, focused, impactful statements that prove why you are the person for the job.

You read Step 1, so you know how to structure an impact statement. Not every impact statement needs a story to be engaging.

If you have read Steps 1-5 and think that an older job in your career will prove you're right for a position, go back about 10-15 years on your resume with responsibilities and impact.

Add leadership impact statements only for positions older than 10-15 years, with no responsibilities. And don't add explanations.

If you worked for a globally recognized company over 15 years ago, put the company name, headquarters location, title, and impact statements. Do not include tasks. That's it. No dates, no company descriptions, and nothing else for positions over a decade ago.

The hiring team can surmise your career story from your resume and LinkedIn profile information, so leave that to them. You just make your statements.

Myth #5: Fulfilling Job Requirements Equals Achievement

If you are an event planner and you planned and executed a successful event, you did your job, nothing more. The event is not an accomplishment or an impact; you did what you were paid to do.

If you're a writer and someone assigned you the goal of 30 articles in one year, and you completed that goal, that is good for you, but that is not necessarily an achievement. However, if some or all of your articles won awards, that is an achievement. If you wrote more than any other writers, that is an achievement. If the articles increased website traffic or circulation, that's even better impact.

Fulfilling job requirements and achieving company goals do not impact the job; they are mandatory parts of the job. If you have questions, go back and review Step 1.

Myth #6: Adjectives and Self-descriptions Are Helpful

Review Step 2 if you still believe this.

Remember that adjectives and self-descriptions are unreliable because most of your competition will claim the same positive traits as you (i.e., great communicator, passionate, self-starter, entrepreneurial, hard worker, etc.). If you use an adjective or describe something helpful about yourself, be prepared to prove it with an impact statement or result. Otherwise, it's pretty useless.

Myth #7: Soft Skills Are Personality Traits

One of the biggest confusions in resume writing and interview prep is soft skills. Almost everyone associates soft skills with personality. One of my esteemed colleagues, J.T. O'Donnell of Work It Daily, once wrote in a LinkedIn post: "… soft skills are typically personality descriptors."

No. Soft skills have nothing to do with personality. Soft skills are people skills and lead to impact like:

- Increase revenue
- Solve problems
- Influence decisions
- Team productivity
- Compliance and policy improvements

Soft skills are behavior and communication skills. It doesn't matter whether you're the commander who wants to lead when you walk in the room or the silent geek in the corner who hides during meetings and wants to sit in her basement office to write code 24/7. Both soft skills are crucial to the company. Each soft skill is important, has its place, and makes its contribution. They're all simply different contributions.

Soft skills are not about your values, morals, environment, or family. Soft skills don't indicate your hard work or your passion. They simply help clarify the type of work you want and help you find the right job and company culture.

I am a licensed behavior analyst. I use DISC methodology, which stands for Dominance, Influence, Steadiness, and Conscientiousness, via digital assessments to help clients discover their strengths and unique soft skills. However, any assessment (Myer Briggs, StrengthsFinder, Predictive Index, Colors) can do this. I discourage you from trying to figure out soft skills on your own because you will probably head toward personality traits or the descriptors from that rejection list and that won't be as helpful.

Use the QR code to contact me for more information about using DISC assessments to find a job and a working environment that suits you.

When asked about soft skills, everyone talks about communication, management, leadership, and attention to detail because they know nothing else. As you have read in Step 1, these traits are not helpful.

Let's discover your natural and unique soft skill strengths together!

COMMON RESUME MISTAKES

For fun, I asked ChatGPT for a sarcastic list of good executive resume requirements. Here's what it gave me:

1. A good resume is completely irrelevant to the position, has typos and grammatical errors, is several pages long, and is filled with irrelevant information, like your passion for knitting or your collection of rare feathers.

2. Use a generic template because clearly, you want to blend in with all the other candidates.

3. Include every job you've ever had, even if it's unrelated to the executive position you're applying for, like when you worked at the ice cream shop in high school.

4. Don't bother proofreading or getting a second opinion because who needs that hassle?

5. Use a non-professional email address, like partyanimal@gmail.com.

6. Include your political views, even if they are completely irrelevant to the job.

Now, you are probably giggling and thinking, *That's so silly! I would never do this.* And yet, I see people do these silly things every day. We can break these down into two categories: resume quality and professionalism.

Have you ever sent your resume to apply for a position you're not sure is right for you? Have you ever considered a position that included a task that you hate doing or at a location where you don't want to live? Have you ever given your resume to a recruiter who said they're not sure about a position, but they're going to send it anyway to see if it "sticks?" Then you're guilty of #1.

Have you ever used one resume to apply for every position? How many? 30? 50? 150? 300? 500? I know for a fact that everyone who is reading this has done so because this is a very popular methodology. It's so much easier! My clients usually send their resumes to hundreds of companies before contacting me. Not surprisingly, they hear from zero. Maybe you'll be luckier. But you are guilty of #2. And I recommend reviewing Step 2.

How far back does your resume go? High school? Your first job as a salesperson at the Gap? (I was guilty of that one years ago.) If you include jobs older than 15 years ago, your resume may be longer than two pages. Then you're guilty of #1 and #3.

If your resume contains a typo—I've seen typos in the job title, in the name of a company, even in the person's name—I think this one speaks for itself, but you're guilty of #4. Take the time to proofread. It's worth the hassle. We agree that it's best to have no typos in anything you send.

Do you use an AOL email address? Do you use an email address that is nicknamed BigSue@hotmail or that represents an opinion like lovemydog@yahoo? Then you've committed #5.

Have you ever assumed the political slant of a company in an email or a cover letter? For example, "I see you want someone with experience supporting DE&I. I would love to join such a liberal company!" Then you have committed #6.

Regarding using AI, I saw a video (posted by a random man) that showed how to copy and paste an entire job description into an AI program to create a resume and cover letter. Forget that he reminded people to "check your work." Forget that hundreds of people commented on how awesome that was. Forget that the resulting resume and cover letter were total junk. The funniest part of this is the fact that people who do this actually think that the hiring team *can't tell*. We can.

So, the two big takeaways here? Don't use AI programs alone to build your resume and don't giggle at others' mistakes because you're probably making the exact same ones.

Go F Your Resume

According to a study by the Neilsen Norman Group[2] in 2006, most recruiters read resumes in an F-shaped pattern. Figure 7 below exemplifies this.

Figure 7 - F-Scan

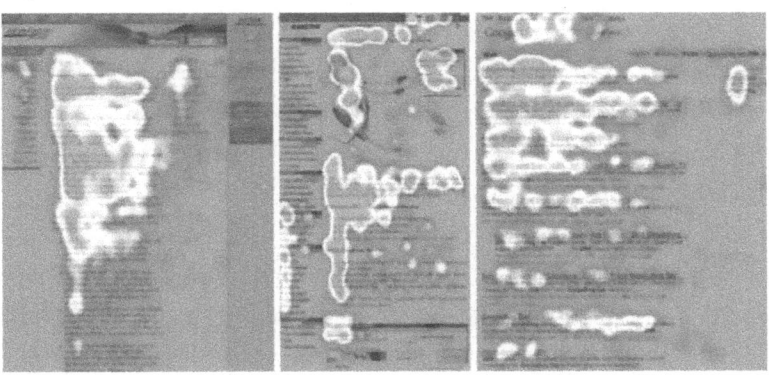

---

[2] Neilsen Norman Group, Retrieved December 22, 2024 from https://www.nngroup.com/articles/f-shaped-pattern-reading-web-content/

Like a radar scan, the densest shaded areas in the images represent the places of most attention, where the recruiters' eyes go most often and spend the most time reviewing.

In all three examples, the densest shaded areas concentrate on the skills and the current or most recent experience. I have been telling my clients for years that the hiring team makes decisions about resumes based on their question: What have you done for us (the field) lately? This F-scan Theory proves that.

To better understand this, scan this QR code to see these images in color.

As I mentioned in this book, most resumes are difficult to read, and it's even more challenging to determine if someone is a good candidate. For example, in the skills section (the bottom tine of the F), all marketing candidates will put some form of social media, advertising, or marketing strategy.

But what differentiates them from other candidates if the skills on all resumes are the same or similar? I'll tell you what sets them apart: Using the keywords from the job posting and showing impact in the most recent positions. The F-scan Theory is further proof of its importance. Because your skills are more or less the same as your competition, what you put in the skills section and the most recent positions is crucial.

The F-scan also proves that your resume doesn't need to be longer than two pages. If you are focusing the title, summary, skills, and the first one to two jobs in your Experience section on the job that you're applying to, and that's where the hiring team has focused their attention, then you don't need more space.

You know how to state what you do or have done. But not everyone can demonstrate results. What did you do with your skills that makes you different? How did you use the same skills everyone else has to impact the company? That's your differentiator. That's what gets you hired.

This F-scan Theory was further proven by an updated scan test in 2019. Look at the updated scan image, Figure 8 below.

Figure 8 - F-Scan Examples

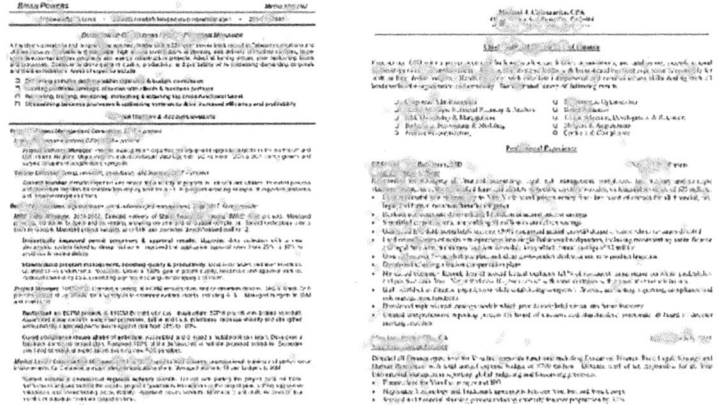

Do you see where the spots have a tiny core of more dense black, especially on the right side sample? That means heavy and repeated concentration. They're all at the top.

Again, to better understand this, scan this QR code to see these images in color.

Go "F" your resume.

The Hiring Side

If you are looking for a job, it is important to understand what it's like on the hiring side of the desk.

Let's pretend for a moment that you're a recruiter. Let's say that you have several positions to fill, and one of them is Vice President of Lending. There is a job posting online for this, and the hiring manager has been quite active on LinkedIn, so several resumes in the applicant tracking system (ATS) are ready to be reviewed. You're lucky because some ATSs don't have search engines, so you'd have to review every resume.

In the ATS, you search for "lending," and two entries appear. *Cool*, you think, *I've narrowed it down already!* But then you look at both resumes, and they're disappointing. One has the word "lending" in the Experience section, so only one is mentioned. The other has the word "lending" under Education—something about a training session. Then you discover they were both submitted a while ago. So, they might not even be pertinent anymore.

So you do another search, this time for "Vice President." Maybe someone in the system at least has executive experience in the financial sector.

One resume comes up, and it says Vice President somewhere near the top. That's it—Vice President. So, you want to dig a little deeper. You know the position you're filling requires Excel because it's in the job posting, and you've spoken to the hiring manager. She knows that everyone at the company uses Excel to track everything—projects and people. So now you search within that resume for "Excel," but it only turns up in the Experience section, in the second position down, which ended five years ago, and it says, "Used Excel."

So you have a decision to make. Should you take the time to have a phone conversation with this candidate, knowing that it might waste up to 20 minutes of your time, or do you email the person, with the understanding that the person's response may not be clear and therefore the email chain will grow very quickly? Or should you just mark the resume for the ever-growing "maybe" list?

Most resumes are poorly written and, therefore, difficult to read. This means it's difficult to determine if a candidate is someone who you should speak to. Remember, there are hundreds of other candidates for this position, and more are coming every day. You will have to do this search repeatedly until you have some decent candidates to consider.

This explanation of the recruiter's experience demonstrates why making each section of the resume impactful is so important. Each section is essential in its own way and worthy of explanation. After reading the above description, I'm sure you'll agree that you want to make it easier for the recruiter to choose you.

Job Boards

Job boards like Indeed, Glassdoor, Monster, WellFound, FlexJobs, and Google are also sources of jobs, but they are different from LinkedIn because they do not have a networking aspect. You may see specific job postings replicated in two or more of these sites, which is the hiring company's attempt to find as many applicants as possible.

Each job board offers free and paid subscriptions/memberships for posting jobs, ATS features, and candidate outreach, so when you apply for a job, you have no idea what the hiring side is seeing or how they are using their membership.

Some technical jobs you think would have many technical requirements will instead have vague instructions (i.e., "Do a good job!"). Some assistant jobs you think would be vague will be filled with specific requirements (i.e., "Don't apply unless you are proficient in Advanced Excel.") There's nothing you can do about this.

If a job posting looks odd or weird to you, someone may have written it who has no idea about your field or the company. Or it was written by an intern with zero experience. Or the hiring manager and HR didn't communicate properly. The bottom line is you don't know who has written the posting.

That job posting on that job board is the only information you have for your job application. I suggest that you milk it for all it's worth.

Changing Your Resume Title

Not all job titles are created equal.

Noelle, the Salesforce software expert, was triple-certified in the Salesforce platform. During one job search, we came across three job titles: Business Analyst, Account Manager, and Salesforce Specialist.

All three job descriptions were similar and were about helping the company use Salesforce to grow and organize sales. After explaining to Noelle that job titles vary wildly, I showed her that changing the title on the resume and adjusting the skills section for each application can make the difference between being noticed and being ignored.

I advise my clients to look beyond the title and thoroughly read every job posting they think they might like. As I indicated earlier, a Vice President of Programs for a local non-profit will be very different than a Vice President of Programs for a global software company. The title is the same but will require very different skills and expertise.

All job descriptions are not the same. Even C-Suite titles differ. If you see eight job postings that all say CEO or Chief Executive Officer, that does not mean all eight companies need the same experience. Yes, they all need leadership and will require a certain amount of experience and expertise in managing people and setting the mission and strategy. But that's where the similarities end. One CEO job might require ten years of experience in toy manufacturing. Another might need at least two years of (working) experience in a physical rehabilitation facility.

The resume's job title is your first impression for the hiring team. The title is at the top, preferably in bold and all caps, so it immediately catches attention and makes a statement. If your title is the title of the job posting, then your first impression will be engaging and positive. Most resumes don't have a title, so upon seeing your focused title, the hiring team will think, *Finally, someone who gets what we need.*

Think about it. If you open a resume for a Marketing Associate role and the title is Marketing Associate, that would give you a great first impression. But what if the role was Marketing Associate, and you open the resume and the title says Marketing Manager? It feels a little off-putting and dampens the first impression.

Please read further than the job title to determine if the job is right for you. Read the entire job description from top to bottom and then determine if the title pertains to you. If the job is right for you, add their title. This will save you and the hiring team a lot of wasted time.

Displaying Your Education

First, displaying your education is not the most important part of your resume, even for an advanced degree.

I know that you're very proud of that MBA or PhD, and I know you worked hard for it. You earned it so you could move up in your industry. Well done, it will help you! And you may talk about that MBA or PhD during an interview or an association meeting. But it's not the most important part of your resume.

If you're in technology, I know you're very proud of all your certifications. However, as proud as you are and as much work as you put into getting them, they are not the most important part of your resume.

You should relegate your education and all those fantastic credentials to the bottom of your resume. They are just as searchable at the bottom of your resume as at the top.

Your real-world experience is much more important (and hopefully more impressive) than your education at any stage of your career. Putting your education at the bottom helps check off some job posting criteria. Most job postings contain some kind of baseline education requirement, usually, at minimum, an associate's or bachelor's degree. But many job postings now say they will accept equivalent/relevant job experience instead of that degree.

There are also plenty of companies, particularly new tech companies, that don't care about where you went to school. This is a counter-culture attitude; they are railing against the social construct. They only care about what your experience offers them—what can you do for them? What have you done lately in your field that will benefit them?

When I help companies with recruiting, sometimes they will put a degree as a requirement, but it's never the sole requirement or even the first requirement—it's always listed in the middle of skills or at the end. They want the degree plus tools, and they always, I mean, *always* want soft skills, even for the most technical of positions.

If you're an executive, your education is the least important part of your application. To compensate for your education being at the bottom, you can add the acronym for the advanced degree and/or certifications next to your name at the top. For example: Soozy Miller, MBA or Soozy Miller, CPRW, CDCC, CDP.

Yes, some companies will only hire alumni of certain schools. That is unavoidable. Ellen, one of my advertising executive clients, was frustrated because she couldn't apply to some top ad agencies; they required graduates from specific schools. But that means you can eliminate those companies immediately, thus further focusing your attention on where you will be more successful.

If you're trying to transition to another career, you might think that the advanced degree is the tool you should emphasize on your resume to make the transition. However, other more effective and impactful ways exist to use the resume. For example, the transferable soft skills and leadership skills are more crucial.

The only exceptions to this education at the bottom recommendation are if you're looking for a job in academia or applying to be in a management or degree program. In those cases, your education goes up top. For everyone else, they place education at the bottom of the resume.

So, shout about your new (or old) education credentials from the top of the mountain—boast about them on all your social media platforms. Go crazy! But when it comes to your resume, put aside your pride and add your education, certifications, and training at the bottom of the resume. It will still check off a requirement box, and your real-world experience and expertise will be seen first, which is the best way to promote you.

Displaying Your Awards on Your Resume

There are two types of awards: Company or organization-specific and general public. The type of award(s) determines where on the resume you should put it so that the award(s) promotes you in the best possible way.

As I stated before, regardless of the type of award, even if the award is not related to your industry, you want to start your resume summary with "Award-Winning." Here are a few more of my recommendations:

- If you received a public award from a non-profit for volunteering, add a Volunteer Work section to the bottom of your resume and put the volunteer work on one line and the award on the following line.

- If you received two or more awards from a non-profit, regardless of what the awards are for, add an Awards section at the bottom of your resume and list the awards.

- If you received one internal award from a well-known company, like the Oracle Customer Service Award, make sure that you add that as an impact statement under the job. Then, add an Awards section at the bottom of your resume and put that award there.

- If you received two or more internal awards from a well-known company, like the Oracle Customer Service Award and the Oracle Business Development Award, make sure that you add those as impact statements under the job in the Experience section and then add an Awards section at the top of your resume under the Summary (above skills) and list those awards there.

- If you received two or more awards from an association connected to your field, add an Awards section at the top of your resume under the summary and above the skills and list those awards there.

Volunteer Work vs. Hobbies and Interests

Job seekers are eager to please the hiring managers and are often so desperate to figure out what the hiring managers want from them that they will do some things that could deter their application.

One popular tactic is adding Hobbies and Interests at the bottom of the resume. While this might catch the interest of some (a fellow snowboarder!), I recommend volunteer work if you have room to spare on your resume.

Let me explain why volunteer work is better. Let's say you go with Hobbies and Interests and put snowboarding. If the interviewer is a skier, that might cause a slight negative subconscious bias. When I used to ski, many fellow skiers complained that snowboarders were rude and reckless with their maneuvers down the mountain. I still remember that loud *thud!* that would happen when a snowboarder landed from a jump because it sounded like someone had fallen. This caused many skiers to lose concentration when they looked around to see who was hurt.

Let's say you go with Hobbies and Interests and put "making pottery." If I tried pottery and could never quite get it, that might also cause a negative subconscious bias. Also, it's messy and super creative, not corporate.

This is why volunteer work is the best resume filler. Regardless of the type of volunteer work, it feeds the soul, so it's impressive. It doesn't invoke any bias, and the hiring team won't find fault with it, even if the work seems a little wacky, like "cleared ski trails" or "hamster adoption." It also shows that you think outside of yourself to the surrounding community. Also, if the interviewer has a friend or relative who did similar volunteer work or volunteered for the same organization, then volunteer work can be a great icebreaker to start a conversation in an interview.

The difference between Hobbies and Interests and Volunteer Work is a thin line. If you prefer hobbies and interests because you haven't done any volunteer work, go with that.

No Links in a Resume

Please don't add links to your resume. Some people will add a company's website address on their resume next to the company name because they're nervous that the hiring team won't be able to research the company if it's small. Don't worry; the recruiter and hiring team will find the company if needed. Please do not add a link to a website.

If you're dying to show off parts of your portfolio that could make or break your application, please don't add the link to your resume. Those links can sit comfortably in your LinkedIn profile. Or you can add the link in an email when contacting a specific contact. If the hiring manager or recruiter wants to see your stuff, they will ask you separately for samples or ask if you have a portfolio site.

Many resume writers and career services coaches will tell you to make your email and LinkedIn addresses live links. The thinking goes: If the recruiter or hiring team likes your resume, they won't have to waste any time; they can just click the links and quickly get in touch with you. I assure you the hiring team will find a way to reach you if they like your resume or LinkedIn profile. Any scenario that you can think of in which a link would help your job application doesn't help you at all.

Some older applicant tracking systems (ATS) have issues with links and will demote your resume in the queue or substitute a bunch of characters for the link, corrupting your document.

Even the most technologically advanced companies might use older ATS systems that don't know how to read a link. One client told me that a global tech company instructed him to send a basic text file version of his resume to apply for a position because their ATS notoriously couldn't read anything else, and his colleagues were easily reaching hiring managers this way. This means that the application technology at this company was so old that it couldn't even read a Word file. While I don't believe that a basic text file was the way to go (a stable Word document would have gotten through just fine), I have observed that even the most advanced global companies will skimp on talent sourcing and go the cheap route regarding hiring. I see that all the time.

Some company systems have security firewalls that could prevent your resume from getting to the ATS if they detect a link. Even if you follow the application process in the job posting, the company's firewall might detect a link to an unrelated site, label it a threat, and reject your resume. Plus, half the time you'll be submitting a PDF document, and depending on the ATS capabilities, the links may or may not be viable.

See that your gorgeous new resume, with its value-add and expertise splendidly outlined, gets noticed. To help ensure this, no links on a resume.

Make the ATS Work for You

The ATS is a very frustrating topic. As we have covered, the Applicant Tracking System (ATS) is the software companies use to qualify candidates for an open position. Job seekers don't understand how it works, and they get frustrated when they never hear from a job application or get a generic rejection letter within minutes or hours. I want to help you understand how the ATS works so that you can make it work for you.

The ATS is usually the first gatekeeper at a company. It is a computer binary system; you're in or out. Someone on the hiring team can automate searches for skills, set acceptance parameters (i.e., years of experience must add up to a minimum), or use the search bar to manually find people with specific skills. Either way, as discussed earlier, if you don't have the skills the hiring team is searching for, you're out, even if you're perfect for the job.

Companies regularly try to fill and re-fill positions, and there are hundreds of candidates (sometimes thousands) for every empty spot. Hiring is a difficult and exhausting task.

This is an example of an ATS screen that a recruiter or someone on the hiring team looks at every day:

Figure 9 - Hiring Team ATS Screen

List Name	PHP Developers in MN	Last Updated	07-02-12 (1:37 pm)
Notes	Dynamic list of candidates in MN with the keyword "PHP" in their resume.	Created By	Tony S.

	Name	Location	Updated ▾	Rating	Recent Status - Extended
☐ 🔍	Sathya Harlesh (View Details)	minneapolis, MN	07-02-12	☆☆☆☆	Submit for review - Java Developer - ACME Enterpri
☐ 🔍	Andrew Kandels	Richfield, MN	07-02-12	★★★★	No Contact - SCUBA Instructor
☐ 🔍	Matt Ingram		07-02-12	☆☆☆☆	No Contact - Website Applicant - Java Developer - A
☐ 🔍	Richard Stevenson	Minneapolis, MN	06-27-12	★★★☆	Contacted - SCUBA Instructor
☐ 🔍	Janet Brooks	Minneapolis, MN	06-27-12	☆☆☆☆	Contacted - Weight Exerciser
☐ 🔍	Greg Battarfield	Minneapolis, MN	06-27-12	☆☆☆☆	No Contact - Weight Exerciser
☐ 🔍	Bob Fullerson	Minneapolis, MN	06-14-12	★★☆☆	No Contact - Weight Exerciser
☐ 🔍	Adam Carleton	Minneapolis, MN	06-07-12	★★☆☆	No Contact - SCUBA Instructor
☐ 🔍	Dorota Konarzewska	Duluth, MN	04-24-12	☆☆☆☆	No Contact - SCUBA Instructor
☐ 🔍	Rachel Donalds	Minneapolis, MN	04-24-12	☆☆☆☆	Contacted - .NET Developer - ABC Siding
☐ 🔍	John Harper	Minneapolis, MN	04-24-12	☆☆☆☆	No Contact - SCUBA Instructor
☐ 🔍	Paul Giggings	Minneapolis, MN	04-20-12	★★★☆	No Contact - Weight Exerciser
☐ 🔍	Paul Johnson	Richfield, MN	09-19-11	☆☆☆☆	Hired - .NET Developer - ABC Siding
☐ 🔍	Kevin Juniper	Saint Paul, MN	07-26-11	☆☆☆☆	Not in Consideration - .NET Developer - ABC Siding
☐ 🔍	Anonymous Candidate	Minnetonka, MN	07-26-11	★★☆☆	Hired - .NET Developer - ABC Siding

Use this QR code to see this image up close.

ATS's are designed to help weed out unqualified people from unrelated fields.

Hiring suffers when companies go the cheap route and under-spend on this software. Cheaper, older ATS software is not up to doing everything needed. And there are repercussions from this.

One repercussion is applicant frustration. Did you ever apply for a job by uploading your resume, only to reach the next page and find that the system incorrectly parsed your information into a form? And then you have to correct all the details? It feels like you're writing your resume all over again. That is an example of an older (legacy) or cheaper system. Whereas the latest software can read crayons written on a paper bag, older systems sometimes can't read Word documents.

This is not a reflection of the company culture or whether you're a good candidate, but it's a total turnoff. To ensure that my job application techniques still work with today's technology, I apply for jobs on a semi-regular basis. I learn something new every time, but when I encounter a legacy system like this, I immediately stop, log out, and close the window.

On the other side of the ATS, life is just as frustrating for the recruiters and hiring team. Most of the time the software reads (scans) the resumes as they come in. If the software doesn't understand something on the resume (e.g., formatting or graphics), the software will either put in substitute characters or rank your resume at the bottom of the list. The hiring team sees the queue on the screen, but sometimes, the handler doesn't even know how to use the software or use it most effectively.

I worked with one Human Resources executive who told me that she regularly trolled the ATS trash for candidates. So, the application process is complicated on both sides of the hiring desk. And the software that is supposed to help sometimes doesn't.

Do you want to get past the ATS to a person? Review Step 2 to tailor your resume to the position.

One recent development in ATS technology is the job board AI review option. As of the end of 2024, two or three U.S. states have made it mandatory for those companies to offer candidates an AI resume review option before they apply for a job. If you see a job posting that you like, you can simply upload your resume using the Review with AI option, and you will quickly receive an AI-based review of your resume compared to the job posting. This option has many problems; however, it can be a great guide and learning tool if you're willing to take the time to learn from each application.

When my clients are having trouble landing interviews, we meet to compare a job posting to the resume they submitted. They quickly learn what they did right and where they fell short. They land a lot more interviews afterward. Contact me at soozy@controlyourcareer.net to see if this issue keeps you from landing interviews.

The AI review option provides this same lesson.

I said that there are many problems with AI. One problem is that AI causes as many problems as it solves. This is particularly true regarding how AI reads the skills section of your resume compared to the skills listed in the job posting. As of 2024, AI is also still very poor at identifying and acknowledging soft skills and leadership impact, how they match up with a job posting, and how soft skills and leadership impact address the needs of the job posting. Computer systems can only use and read binary code; AI is not human, it's data-based knowledge. Therefore, even the most advanced AI systems cannot compare human achievements to words listed in a job posting.

For example, let's say a job posting you like requires "expert knowledge of Advanced Excel," and you forgot to add Advanced Excel in the skills section of your resume. However, your Experience section contains an impact statement: "Increased sales by 30% by directing sales team to develop shareware and coordinate reporting systems such as Excel." The AI review may not necessarily read your achievement as pertinent to the position (Advanced Excel vs. Excel), even though the impact statement proves you're probably a better candidate than 99% of the other applicants.

The human element is where machines fall short.

If you're applying to a manufacturing executive position, you probably don't need to put that you're an expert at Microsoft Word. While I have seen one or two (out of thousands) executive job postings that put Microsoft Word as a requirement, usually for an executive position the company is looking for leadership in mission and strategy.

Regardless of how much you want the job or think that you deserve the job, the fact is that the ATS could keep your resume from being seen by anyone at all. Failing to tailor your title, summary, and skills section to the specific job, as suggested in Step 2, reduces your chances of being seen.

If you focus your title, summary, and skills sections on the company's needs, your chances of being seen in the ATS increase. I wish I could call this a hack or a trick and say that's the key, but it's never that simple. This just increases your chances.

So, yes, the ATS is usually part of the process. For now, companies must use them—or else they just can't keep up with the barrage of job seekers. You might as well get used to the ATS and use my methods to make it work for you.

The Dreaded Cover Letter

The cover letter is on its way out of the hiring process, kicking and screaming as it goes.

The cover letter is the most talked about topic in the career services field. It is a hotly debated and very polarizing issue.

I was in a meeting with some executive recruiters and executive career coaches. An HR executive with decades in the industry said, "My colleagues and I have nothing to do with cover letters. We don't ask for them, and we don't write them."

An executive coach responded, "I love cover letters. They help me with candidates."

Sigh.

To exemplify how awkward the cover letter conversation can be, I once watched an interview with an internationally known executive career coach. At one point, the interviewer said, "Now we're going to talk about the dreaded topic of cover letters."

My colleagues say they either love cover letters and encourage their clients to keep using them or hate cover letters and wish they would go away. I'm in the latter camp. I hate cover letters. I think they're a waste of time and energy.

The funny thing is, historically speaking, the cover letter was the original resume. Hundreds of years ago, if you wanted a job, like an apprenticeship, you would write a letter to a company requesting employment.

Now, only about 50% of applications call for a cover letter. Google led the way in 2022 when they stopped requiring cover letters in applications.

If a job application does not ask for a cover letter, don't send one; it means that they don't want to see one, they just want the resume. Don't try to get around this, and don't try to beat your competition by attaching your cover letter to your resume as one big document. That is a turnoff.

When I'm in the recruiter role, the resume tells me everything I initially need to know.

However, some companies still want to see them. Some recruiters think the cover letter is a great way to get to know the candidate. A recruiter or hiring manager may also use the cover letter to see who puts in that extra effort to reduce the applicant pile.

One executive recruiter told me that when four Senior Vice Presidents were up for the same job, and it was time to eliminate one, the company used one of the candidates' lack of a cover letter as a reason to omit him. That's how much all of the candidates looked alike.

People think they must write about their entire lives to sell themselves in the cover letter. People may think that many things on the resume need to be explained further and contextualized, and the cover letter is the place to do that. You want to be careful here. The cover letter can be an asset when it's well written.

Here are some tips for writing an engaging, enticing, and effective cover letter:

- Lots of white space.
- One or two short-sentence paragraphs at the top explaining how you can address the company's needs as outlined in the job posting.
- Three bullet point accomplishments/value-add statements from your resume that address the company's needs.

Do not make these bullet points about self-descriptions, skills, or actions.

- One final paragraph thanking the company for taking the time to read the cover letter and resume.

That's it. Plain, simple, and to the point.

Think of the cover letter as a way to get the hiring team excited about the resume. The cover letter is a preview document. At its best, the cover letter simply encourages the hiring team to check out your resume.

Don't spend hours on a cover letter; spend minutes. Even if the job application requires a cover letter, that does not mean that someone will read it.

Start Your Job Search on LinkedIn

If you want to know where to start your job search, start on LinkedIn.

As mentioned earlier, LinkedIn has over 1 billion members in more than 220 countries. And while a portion of those profiles may not be very active, you still have numbers on your side.

Think about how much easier and faster your job search would be if you were already actively connecting with hundreds (or thousands!) of people who could link you to your next opportunity. Even if you have hundreds of personal connections in the business world, you want to be connected on LinkedIn to extend your reach even further.

For those who have not used LinkedIn or have only used it a little, networking on LinkedIn is a great starting point.

First, make sure that your LinkedIn profile is optimal. We discussed this earlier in Step 3.

Second, make as many connections as you can:

- Find and talk to recruiters in any field you're interested in pursuing.
- Research companies you're interested in.
- Find, connect, and communicate with executive leaders of those companies.
- Connect with people who will then introduce you to a specific person you'd like to talk to.
- Engage in conversations about topics in your field and show that you're good at what you do.

If you subscribe to LinkedIn Premium, you can see who has been visiting your profile and then choose who you want to contact to start a conversation.

The best way to reach out and connect with people you don't know, barely know, or haven't spoken to in a long time is to use the information from Steps 1 and 2, impact and addressing need, to engage with them.

Don't write this:

Hi Samantha, Do you have any jobs available? I believe that I have the skills and experience to work in [field]. I've been working in [field] for about three years and I like the job, but the company has told us they are going to lay off a bunch of people. Any help would be greatly appreciated!

Instead, before you reach out, look at the company's profile online or the job posting if you're interested or applying for a specific job. After you address the person, you can go right into acknowledging the need you see and proving that you have addressed that need and made the company better.

Write this instead:

> Hi Samantha, I see you are a [position] for [Company]. I applied to the [position title] because I see they need help with monitoring daily auditing. When I was at [previous company], I oversaw auditing and found some issues that we immediately addressed. I saved [previous company] $100K in fines and the associated internal complications.

See the difference?

Then, after you have connected with people and gotten the attention of some appropriate people, you can adjust your resume to any opportunities they have available or know of.

Your LinkedIn profile is always public and global, so it is meant to be your self-promotion.

Many features like searches, text, and suggested connections can help you network. Once I show clients how to use LinkedIn, they understand its usefulness and potential.

So, start your job search on LinkedIn. Once you get more comfortable and can harness its power, you will start to control your career.

Contact me (soozy@controlyourcareer.net) if you'd like more information about how to make LinkedIn work for you!

Marketing Yourself

You might see the header here and think, *I need a resume. What does marketing have to do with it? Are you suggesting that I hire a publicist?*

To significantly reduce your job search time, you want to show how you're different from your competition and how you can address the company's needs. That's marketing.

You've probably heard the term "personal branding," but you have no idea what that is and where to start. Personal branding is just another term for reputation. Reputation is about demonstrating to the world your unique value-add and expertise. Just like companies market their products so that more people buy them, we want to market your unique leadership strengths, expertise, and value-add so that more companies you like want to buy (hire) you at the price (salary) you deserve. When you differentiate yourself from your competition and make it clear why you are the better choice, they have no choice but to hire you instead of the others.

I once trusted a company and got burned with no results. I paid about $1K to an AI company because a friend worked there, and I trusted her expertise. However, they simply swamped LinkedIn with typo-filled messages, and I never got any clients. I learned that I must own my strategy by researching and asking better questions to see if that strategy will address my needs.

The cool thing is that using marketing tools didn't just work for me; it worked for all types of clients. Take Oscar. He is an executive chef who was suffering from The Great Resignation. He was overworked and exhausted and needed a new job, but he had no idea how to start. So, he decided to try a career coach. Before we finished his sessions, he told me his phone had been "ringing off the hook" with fantastic offers.

What did Oscar do differently? Oscar learned how to market himself to his industry using his new materials. Instead of sending his resume everywhere, he learned to target the right jobs and then demonstrate why he was the best choice. He learned to write and speak about himself in a way that attracted better opportunities to him instead of chasing them. That's marketing.

The best way to look for a job is by incorporating marketing techniques. The marketing aspect of your job search is crucial for making you stand out from your competition.

Control your career by branding your expertise, demonstrating what makes you the better choice, using your impact to address the company's needs, and matching that information to the perfect job.

Recruiters vs. Career Coaches

Many people complain on LinkedIn about recruiters, executive recruiters, the hiring team, and the lack of feedback about why they didn't land the job. They wrongly mistake recruiters for coaches.

Recruiters and hiring teams are not career coaches. They have no obligation to the job seeker about career advice or resume feedback, no matter how high up the corporate ladder you are.

I am both a recruiter and a career advisor. These are two very different positions with almost no crossover. The only activity that they have in common is reading resumes. However, the recruiter and the career advisor read resumes for different reasons.

As a recruiter, because there are so many applicants (usually 150+ for each open position), I am very picky about who I interview because interviews take up a lot of time. Usually, resumes are so poorly written that I have to read between the lines to figure out or guess if the person has the skills and tools to do the job. And reading the resume is just the beginning. Then, I will go to LinkedIn to see if more information can help me. If not, sometimes I will email the candidate for more information. For instance, if I'm hiring for a marketing manager position, and the job posting calls for experience posting on Instagram, but the resume only says Social Media, I will email the candidate to ask if they have experience posting business content on Instagram. Sometimes, the candidate will reply with a screenshot of a posting, and it's from their personal account, not a business posting. So then I have to decide if I still want to pursue this.

So before we spend time in an interview, we recruiters also need to figure out if the person has leadership skills and fits the company culture. It's a hard no 90% of the time.

As a recruiter, I receive about 25 applications per day per position. I often have 2-3 positions to fill. That number might seem low and easy because I've been doing this for 10 years; however, when candidates submit poorly written and formatted resumes, I have to sift through a lot of unnecessary—sometimes repeated—information. And when there are mass layoffs like there have been since December 2022, you can 5X or 10X that number of applications. All the resumes look so alike, and it's mind-numbing.

So, yes, as a recruiter, I use the dreaded generic "thank you for applying" email template as often as possible. I do not have time to compose a customized, special-for-you letter with a resume review to send to each person. Plus—and this is a big consideration—I'd say that up to 98% of resumes come from candidates who don't work in the field.

Once, I was recruited for a marketing manager position and received resumes from IT specialists, event planners, and other unrelated fields. People were throwing their resumes at me, hoping I would find something in their experience to land them work. I could not waste precious time explaining to an IT specialist why they were not right for a marketing management job.

On the other hand, as a career advisor and resume writer, I help clients through this frustrating, exhausting, and stressful process.

- I explain the recruiter and hiring team's thinking process.
- I explain how the ATS works.
- I give my clients constructive feedback about their resume and their LinkedIn profile.
- I successfully prepare my clients for interviews by teaching them interview skills, general best practices, and conducting mock interviews.
- I encourage my clients to apply for appropriate jobs and discourage them from applying for the wrong ones.
- I support my clients so that they reduce their job search stress and anxiety.
- I keep them on the right track.
- I encourage my clients to make mistakes with me so that I can redirect them and make suggested changes.

That is my job as a trusted career advisor. That is not the recruiter's job or the hiring team's job.

My client, Jamie, was getting rejection after rejection, and he didn't know why. "I am completely qualified for these jobs," he told me. "I reached out to the recruiter to ask why, but no one is answering me."

After some conversations about recruiters, resume writers, and coaches, he understood the difference. Also, we figured out that he had been applying for manufacturing jobs when his experience was in operations.

While some recruiters might have extra time and be willing to help you, their feedback can be a liability for them. Also, it's not their job to tell you. That's my job.

Instead, invest a little money in a resume writer or a coach. I guarantee that you'll land the job sooner. And you won't even need feedback from the company.

The Challenge of Adjectives

As previously mentioned, the two major challenges with using adjectives on a resume and LinkedIn profile are that first, everyone uses the exact words "good communicator" and "detail-oriented," and second, no one will believe you. Everyone says they are awesome on a resume and a LinkedIn profile because what else will they say? *I'm mediocre?*

Another one of my favorites is "entrepreneurial—able to work alone or as part of a team." I certainly hope so!

One of the issues here is that people don't dig deeper. There are many more adjectives available. Analytical, risk-taker, persuasive, energetic, competitive, and calming are a few that immediately come to mind. And these can easily be proven with experience.

Each person has different strengths. We're all simply different. Suppose you are more driven and feel comfortable leading meetings, taking risks, and driving the business. In that case, you will use different adjectives to describe yourself than someone who is more analytical, hangs back, and researches data before making a decision. One style of working is not better or worse than the others. All soft skills bring benefits and value to any situation or problem.

How do you relay your unique qualities and describe yourself when it's difficult to differentiate yourself?

My first suggestion is to use a data-backed assessment like DISC. If you can't do this or don't have access, try to prove the adjective you're claiming about yourself. If you must go with "good communicator," then try to prove how your good communication skills benefited and impacted the company. If you use "team player," then at least try to show how being a team player benefited the company.

Even though "communication," "team player," and "results-oriented" are in most job descriptions, recruiters and the hiring team do not search for these words. Companies expect you to communicate with your team, work well with others, and strive for results. Even though these words are in the job description, using these words on your resume is the equivalent of saying that you work with a computer. Or that you can use a desk. Or that you breathe.

However, they might search for "analytical" (or "analytics"), and they might search for "risk-taker" (or "risk") *if the job calls for those skills* because those words are descriptive and helpful.

Look at your impact statements in your resume Experience section and figure out detailed adjectives that best describe your actions. Use a Thesaurus. Just make sure that the adjectives don't stand alone. If you use "successful," then prove that with an impact statement in the Experience section. Remember, success is not just about completing a task. Prove each adjective on your resume and LinkedIn profile by showing how that characteristic benefited past companies.

Otherwise, like the millions of other people vying for the job, you're just a good communicator who prioritizes results by being a team player.

Use this QR code to contact me for further information about using DISC assessments to help your job search.

Want a Promotion?

A manager, Bonnie, was interested in a promotion that opened up at her company. She thought she was right for the job and applied internally for it. When she didn't get the promotion, she was upset and disappointed. So she contacted me to discuss it.

> Bonnie: I deserved that position. I earned it. I should have gotten it.
>
> Me: I understand your frustration. Why do you deserve it?
>
> Bonnie: Because I work hard and have done so much for the company.
>
> Me: Oh! That's good! Tell me three things that you've accomplished for the company.

She couldn't name any. Yet, she still expected to be noticed and promoted.

If you do your job and go home—if you simply fulfill your job requirements and no more—your boss or other leadership will see you as the average worker and probably won't notice you or consider you for other roles. The company is investing in you by paying you a salary, and with that comes expectations— that you will get the job done, of course, but more importantly, that you will somehow make the company better. They hope you will leave the company better than when you arrived, whether or not you're in leadership.

Remember Mary, the event planner? If you planned an event, you did your job. It is irrelevant how hard you worked to make that event a success. Your hard work is expected; it is not an accomplishment. You simply fulfilled your job requirement. You probably won't get attention for that from the boss.

However, if your budget was cut in half, or half your staff quit, or a natural disaster struck (like a tree falling on the venue roof), and the event raised the same amount of money— or better yet, more than the previous event—despite these obstacles, that is an achievement.

An executive event planner, Sally, had a challenging time explaining to me why her work mattered. Whenever I asked her how her work affected others or made a difference, she had no idea what to say. She always answered me with some tasks she had completed. I coached her through this:

Sally: The event in the spring brought in about $85K in donations.

Me: That's excellent. How did you help with that?

Sally: What do you mean? I planned it.

Me: Yes, but was there something you did to facilitate the larger donations?

Sally: I don't know what you mean.

Me: Was there some unique idea you came up with during the event planning that caused people to donate more, thus achieving the $85K?

Sally: Not during the event, but after the event, yes.

Me: Okay, tell me about that.

Sally: I hired a graphic designer and a calligrapher to design special thank-you notes. You know, "Thank you for attending."

With a bit of help, she could demonstrate one very specific way that she brought value. Sally brought in that extra $85K in donations, and she could use that as proof of why she deserved to move up in her field and earn more money.

Remember Gerard, the successful finance director? He wanted a better, higher-paying job with fewer hours. But he couldn't explain anything when I asked him to give me details about his successes.

In one coaching session, I pointed out that he was not the only finance director out there and that if he wanted more control over his situation, he would have to detail his impact. And if he couldn't explain his success to me—the coach who would let him repeatedly try and fail until he got it—he would not get what he wanted. Demonstrating your impact and results is key to more money and moving up in the company.

Are you eyeing a promotion? Do you deserve a better job with better hours and pay?

Your argument that you are loyal, your years of service, passion, and hard work will not get you what you think you deserve.

Get ready to prove what you deserve by detailing your value-add and how your expertise has benefited companies and organizations.

Your Resume and LinkedIn Are Not the Same

Your resume and your LinkedIn profile are not created equal. They are not interchangeable. They support and complement each other, but they are not the same.

My clients Kate and Tim received interviews and job offers straight from their LinkedIn profiles just days after I helped them re-brand and re-write all the content. However, that does not mean their LinkedIn profile was a substitute for their resume.

The resume and the LinkedIn profile are two very different tools with different purposes. The only part the resume and the LinkedIn profile have in common is the Experience section. And even that section has its differences between the two.

Some of my clients decide to forego writing a LinkedIn profile because they want to save money and plan to copy and paste their resume information into LinkedIn. While that improves the LinkedIn profile Experience section a bit, neglecting the headline and About sections can be detrimental to your career advancement.

Here's how and why your resume and LinkedIn profile are different.

The resume is used to land an interview. That's it. It doesn't land you the job or guarantee your salary. You send your resume to a specific contact at a specific company to apply for a specific position or upload it online to apply for a specific job posting. You can refer to Step 2 regarding the benefits of a focused resume.

The LinkedIn profile is your public professional face to the world. Your LinkedIn profile is, therefore, meant to attract attention in a way your resume cannot. People on the hiring side visit LinkedIn for various reasons. Recruiters use LinkedIn in addition to their search software (ATS). Hiring managers go there to search for talent. Human Resources departments with hiring teams go there. Anyone looking to hire a business consultant goes there. Companies looking for alliances and partnerships go there. Even headhunters who look for specific executives to fill specific leadership positions might use LinkedIn for research.

People use LinkedIn for a variety of reasons: networking, business support, topic discussions, learning, and, yes, job search. When you connect with people on LinkedIn, they will visit your profile to see more about you. This means your LinkedIn profile is more of a global catch-all and is better at publicly promoting you than a resume could ever be.

An optimal LinkedIn profile contains a variety of industry and searchable keywords everywhere and makes clear, attractive, engaging statements about your expertise and value-add. When your LinkedIn profile is optimized, it should attract various opportunities.

A good way to use your LinkedIn profile and resume in tandem is to interact on LinkedIn regularly to attract attention to your profile. Then, when an interested party reaches out to you about a specific opportunity, you ask for a job description and then focus your resume as best as possible on that opportunity.

Or, you might get hired straight off your LinkedIn profile because it's so optimized and engaging.

Together, your LinkedIn profile and resume can land you your dream job with your dream salary.

Vive la difference, as they say.

How to Beat 14,000 Applicants

A client, Jan, told me she saw a job posting indicating 14,000 people had applied.

Yes, you read that right: 14,000 applicants.

I think that's the highest I've ever seen.

I told her that the number could be 14, 140, or 14,000; it doesn't really matter in terms of how it affects her job application. True, you might not hear from the company for a while with that number of applicants. They have a lot of skills searches to do and a lot of resumes to review. And, yes, I feel sorry for the recruiters and hiring teams that must go through all those resumes.

However, two things remain constant in job applications: whether you are fresh out of college or a CEO applying for a job, or whether there are four applicants or 14,000.

First, you will stand out from all the applicants if your resume addresses the company's needs and shows your leadership impact and value-add.

Second, about 95-98% of those 14,000 job applications are from unrelated industries. The posting that Jan saw was a marketing leadership position, and I can tell you that people from academia, manufacturing, IT, medicine, finance, and other unrelated industries made up that 95-98%.

Why is that applicant number so high? My guess is LinkedIn Easy Apply. As I've said, it's one of the worst ideas ever. While it appears easy to click Easy Apply and *voila!* you have applied with almost no effort; the resulting application is an ineffective way to apply for a job. I recommend you not do this.

But also, don't be put off by 14,000 applicants. Think of it as 140 or 14. Or even four. The numbers don't matter. If you show you can meet the company's needs and improve it, you will be noticed and someone will contact you.

Be Smart, Not Desperate

Earlier, I talked about reducing your job search time by at least 90%. I recommended methods for reading job descriptions and rejecting most jobs so that you only put your energy into jobs that are appropriate for you so that you don't waste time. Then, I made recommendations for conquering the interview.

If you see someone random on LinkedIn offering advice because they finally landed a job after 500 applications, I suggest you ignore them, even if they have 15,000 followers.

The sample resumes I see from these posters are unreadable and confusing because there is so much unnecessary information that I can't tell what the person does. The formats are so complicated and ornate that they make me dizzy.

People post that they're landing jobs with these unreadable resumes and want to help others. I understand the desire to pay success forward. It is admirable. However, just because you landed a job doesn't mean your process will work for everyone.

If you have a newborn baby, especially if it's your first child, that does not put you in a position to tell other new parents how to raise their children.

If you saw a great movie, that does not put you in a position to tell a director how to make a film.

If you lost weight, that does not put you in a position to tell people how to lose weight.

If you landed a job after 500 applications and 50 interviews, those numbers are way too high, and whatever you did to get the job does not help other people. It makes other people think that 500 applications and 50 interviews are an acceptable path, and that simply is not true. If you optimize your resume and only consider appropriate jobs, you should apply to up to five jobs per week and land 1-6 interviews within 1-3 weeks. Much less stressful. Much more effective.

150 applications and 25 interviews, 500 applications and 50 interviews are not success, people. It's desperation.

Let's be smart about those job applications and interviews. Make sure that your LinkedIn profile demonstrates your talent. Read the job posting and ensure that you match the requirements and that you like the job description, and then plagiarize the job posting for the title, summary, and skills section. During interviews, emphasize and prove how you can address the company's needs.

These methods will empower you, regardless of your circumstances and field. When something goes awry at your job—and something will, at some point—you won't feel desperate and won't have to worry as much about your career.

You have the power to control your own decisions about your future.

If you have further questions, refer to Steps 1-5.

Take control of your career.

AFTERWORD

CHANGE

One last word about change.

To move forward with a better job in a better work culture and to ensure that you feel more control over your career, you want to look back first.

Ask yourself a few questions:

What good and bad things am I leaving behind?

When could I have treated someone better?

What helpful and unhelpful tools will I miss?

What did I forget to make better?

Where did I fall short?

What have I done in the past that might have kept me from my best possible reputation?

What changes do I want to make so this new awesome position will work out?

These are important questions to ask yourself because to be your best possible self at your next job, you want to drop any unhelpful habits and feelings that you carry inside with you. Even your dream job with the best possible salary at the best company is still a change to your schedule, family, and lifestyle. Excellent changes still contain an emotional component. Change is just as emotional as it is situational, external, and physical.

You may not enjoy the best experience possible at the new job if you still carry emotional and physical residual responses from your last job, even if you loved it.

Before you start your new work, take some time during this job search process to ask yourself the questions above. Acknowledge the good and bad aspects that you are leaving behind. Your new job may require or integrate some tools and talents that you bring from your previous experiences, but you still want to acknowledge, accept, and say goodbye to that past part of you.

Any change—good and bad—takes energy. To ensure your best possible you and your best possible future, say goodbye and thank you to your past. Your experience got you where you are today, and now it's time for tomorrow.

ABOUT THE AUTHOR

Soozy Miller is a recruiter, a resume writer, and a career advisor. Her mission is to improve company culture one person at a time and to show you how to control your career until you don't want to work anymore. Her knowledge of executive leadership behavior patterns, hiring software, the hiring lifecycle, and what hiring teams want to see ensures a shorter job search, resulting in more and better job offers. She helps executives shift from stuck to empowered so they feel more in control of their future, feel inspired to be better leaders, and land better-paying jobs in more comfortable work environments.

Soozy is a Certified Master Resume Writer, a Certified DISC Communication & Behavioral Consultant, a Certified DISC Practitioner, and a former Professional Association of Resume Writers & Career Coaches (PARW/CC) member. She has been named a Top 10 Communications Coach by Yahoo Finance. She has appeared on numerous radio shows and has been on Bloomberg, Yahoo News, MatchWatch, Street Insider, and others.

Soozy co-authored the bestselling book *Business Leadership and Culture* (Amazon). She has been a business writer for more than 35 years and has coached hundreds of executives worldwide to control their careers.

Soozy lives in Manhattan, New York, where she enjoys theater, writing, watching great streaming series, and trying new sushi restaurants.

Work with Soozy
Control Your Career

Career Coaching Services

Schedule a call with Soozy and get the job you want, saving yourself time and frustration. Here's what we'll cover in one or two sessions:

- Review your career moves thus far and determine what could hold you back from your next great opportunity. Have you been talking about your impact?

- Determine what you deserve regarding title, working environment, and salary by leveling up your job search. Stop wasting time on inappropriate jobs.

- Feel empowered to apply for jobs that you want. Drastically reduce your job search time.

- Learn the tools and methods to serve you until you don't want to work anymore. You deserve to be in control of your career!

- Coaching through the application and interview process. Save time and make more money.

- Encouragement to get you to the finish line. Don't get stuck in the weeds. Follow the methodology.

Resume Writing Services

What makes a resume successful? What makes a resume bad? Get these answers and feel empowered to use your resume as a powerful tool.

LinkedIn Profile Writing & Strategy Services

Not getting enough attention on LinkedIn? Seeing the wrong kind of attention? This is because your profile is not attractive, and you're sending the wrong messages. Let's bring out your amazing impact and results and send messages that engage instead of repel.

Career Consulting Services

Not sure what you want? Not sure what you need? Let's discuss and discover together. This can be during the job search or before you even start.

Recruitment Services

Control Your Career is proud to partner with You First Solutions, an expert AI recruiter service that enables you to contact thousands of hiring managers and decision-makers. Control Your Career is the only career service providing short-term and long-term career help, job search materials, and job placement in one package.

DISC Profile Assessment Consulting

What is the best type of job for me? What should I do next? How can I speak to my unique strengths? Control Your Career provides an all-encompassing assessment of your strengths and blind spots and a communication plan to help you throughout your career. This helps with interviews and career conversations and helps make you a more inspirational leader in your next position.

What Clients are Saying

Soozy Miller amazed me with her industry insight and brilliant methods of branding myself. She consistently demonstrated her expertise at Control Your Career and a commitment to success. ~Steven, Professor & Executive Business Advisor

I wanted to let you know the phone has been ringing off the hook!!! I'm not sure how some headhunters got my resume, but it's been great. ~Oscar, Executive Chef

When I applied for my first job with my new resume, I received an interview request in four minutes! ~Anand, Director of Medicine

I feel confident about how this job search is going and my incoming success, landing a job that allows me to flex my skills and continue to grow. Words cannot simply explain how much I appreciate you for this feeling. ~Ezekiel, Marketing Executive

It looks like me! Yay! Thank you! Thanks so much, Soozy. I appreciate you listening to me and then integrating your critical expertise and my experience to draft a resume that looks and feels like me and my evolving professional goals. ~Keisha, DE&I Specialist

AWESOME EXPERIENCE! Thank you for taking my skills, accomplishments, and experiences and organizing them into a clear and concise resume. Each time I send my resume, I'm confident I speak directly to the position I'm applying for and consistently get interviews. ~Noelle, Salesforce Executive

Control Your Career

Soozy G. Miller

Soozy@ControlYourCareer.net

www.ingramcontent.com/pod-product-compliance
Lightning Source LLC
Chambersburg PA
CBHW051320120626
46547CB00015B/2315